Win

The Institute of Management (IM) is at the
forefront of management development and
best management practice. The Institute
embraces all levels of management from
students to chief executives. It provides a
unique portfolio of services for all managers,
enabling them to develop skills and achieve
management excellence.

If you would like to hear more about the
benefits of membership, please write to
Department P, Institute of Management,
Cottingham Road, Corby NN17 1TT.

This series is commissioned by the
Institute of Management Foundation.

Winning at Change

How to make change work for you

■ ■ ■

**GEORGE BLAIR AND
SANDY MEADOWS**

PITMAN PUBLISHING
128 Long Acre, London WC2E 9AN

A Division of Pearson Professional Limited

First published in Great Britain 1996

© Pearson Professional Limited 1996

British Library Cataloguing in Publication Data
A CIP catalogue record for this book can be obtained from the British Library.

ISBN 0 273 61595 5

10 9 8 7 6 5 4 3 2 1

Typeset by Northern Phototypesetting Co Ltd, Bolton
Printed and bound in Great Britain by Bell and Bain Ltd, Glasgow

The Publishers' policy is to use paper manufactured from sustainable forests.

Contents

■   ■   ■

About the Authors

■ ■ ■

George Blair is a management consultant who has worked in marketing and human resources management within a wide range of industries before becoming a management consultant, specialising in organizational change. He has chaired national conferences and led workshops on change. He is experienced in both the public and private sectors internationally as well as in the UK, and is also a director of the Manpower Society.

Sandy Meadows is a job share director of a personnel and management consultancy who has 19 years' experience in a variety of general management and human resources roles. She has been involved in developing strategic HR capability in a number of private and public sector settings. She is a national authority on workforce planning and organizational design and is joint author of the *People Pack*, an acclaimed HR strategy and workforce planning manual.

Foreword

■   ■   ■

Is the juggernaut of change speeding towards your organization? You are determined not to be caught in its headlights like a frightened rabbit, but where do you find the time to gear yourself up to become the driver or navigator of the juggernaut? You are already working long hours and are under a great deal of pressure to succeed. May be you have been extremely successful to date, but what is your work atmosphere like now? Does it feel a bit like the Palace of the Medicis where intrigue and backstabbing are the order of the day? Do you wonder whose body will be floating in the river tomorrow morning?

You are aware of the new fads and fashions in organizational change that come and go. Increasingly these are grabbing the attention of chief executives and chairmen and moving to the top of their agendas. Undoubtedly, achievement in organizations now and in the future will be judged on an individual's ability to drive and facilitate change, not in effective command and control as previously. People can no longer look to their organizations for their salvation. You must accept responsibility for your own future development and the attainment of your personal goals.

How are you going to ensure that you will continue to be judged as a high-achiever faced with these new demands? Simple, read this book! We have designed this book to help busy managers like you across all sectors not only to survive but win at organizational change. So how can we justify this claim? For one thing we know what it feels like to be affected by significant change. This has been through first hand experience when as line managers in large, complex companies we had personally to deliver change. We have felt the initial fear and anxiety of wondering whether we were up to the task confronting us, but we discovered ways through and have used the lessons we learnt to assist other managers to thrive on change. This book draws on many books, articles, research papers, conferences, workshops and our own and others' practical experience. We have distilled from these and from our own background working in organizations undertaking significant change programmes those skills needed by tomorrow's manager. Self assessments have been built in so you can judge for yourself whether you have the required skills and if not, how to acquire them.

Surprisingly, nobody has written a handy reference guide to the subject for busy managers who want to grasp the main thrust of the latest management thinking so they can then decide those areas that they want to pursue in greater depth. The authors of change tend to advocate one best way of bringing about change. Either Total Quality Management (TQM) was the answer to your prayers or the only way to succeed was through business process re-engineering. We know the hard way – that there is no one solution.

We do not fly the banner for any particular approach. We give you the key to find the approach most in tune with your organization and achieving your own personal goals. We will help you to find the best approach for you and your organization through checklists and case studies. We will show you how to make the linkages between the various approaches so that you can mix a cocktail for changing your organization. This will consist of those essential ingredients that you have identified as being vital. You will not be constrained by having to select from one particular approach but the potency will come from your ability to mix and match from the vast array of practice available.

We take you through an action planning process that will not only help you to succeed in the face of today's challenges but which will equip you to win at change whenever it confronts you.

Acknowledgements

■ ■ ■

Special thanks to Philip Gill and Stephen Connock for their support throughout the various drafts of the book and in particular for contributing their ideas, experience and articles that they have happened upon in their own work.

We would also like to thank the many people who without knowing it have added to the highly practical nature of this book through freely contributing their time and energy to test a number of our approaches in their own organization.

xiii

The leaders of tomorrow will be those who have seized opportunities that change brings.

1

...

Why change won't go away

International competition · high consumer expectations ·
shorter product life cycles · wider product ranges ·
political change · intellectual obsolescence · end of
conventional career paths

In the past able managers like you have been able to ride out change by being better than average performers. You work hard, you are highly motivated, you achieve all your objectives, you get things done around here. Sadly, these attributes are no longer enough. The pace of change is faster, its impact remorseless. Organizations are delayering, downsizing, outsourcing, ending conventional career paths and rendering some skills and experience obsolete. The winds of change may already be whistling through the corridors of your organization or you may be feeling quietly confident that you have escaped the storm so far. We want to convince you from the outset that change is not going to go away. It is becoming an integral part of everybody's experience. The leaders of tomorrow will be those who have seized opportunities that change brings.

No organization is safe. Like actors we are only as good as our last individual or corporate performance. Previously successful companies like star performers have eclipsed with 71 American companies having slipped off Fortunes top 100 list between 1956 and 1992.[1] Size and power don't give immunity. IBM, once one of the most successful organizations, has made huge losses after many years of large profits. Microsoft, now almost a household name was unheard several years ago. So what are these factors that humble both Davids and Goliaths and facilitate the meteoric rise of others?

International competition

■ ■ ■

This now impacts on every fact of our life. How often have you

[1] *Economist*, 4 April, 1992, page 15.

dreamed of an exotic adventure holiday to an unspoilt paradise on the other side of the world. You have been charmed by the long, empty, sandy beaches, the fascinating local customs and the delicate flavours of the native cuisine. Then, to your shock and horror you are confronted by the jolly face of Colonel Sanders welcoming you to partake of Kentucky fried chicken, just like they make back home. Once you can recover you equilibrium, you should really be congratulating this fine example of total global marketing. Companies such as global fast food chains succeed by being the first to gain a foothold in even the most remote or unlikely location ahead of the competition.

Now close to home, the brand names with which we were once familiar are not all that they seem. Rolls Royces will soon have BMW engines. Rovers, once fully British owned and built, were then made with Honda only to be later taken over by BMW. The Norton motorbike has been swept away in the wake of Kawasakis, Suzukis and Hondas. We have all become accustomed to the designer names such as Chanel, Lacoste and Levi Strauss taking advantage of cheaper labour costs in the Pacific rim for the manufacture of their products. However, they are beginning to lose market share to Asian designers who design and market in their own right.

Other than spoiling an exotic holiday and increasing the range of goods available to you, what does this mean for you?

More quality conscious consumers

Consumers want and expect more choice both in variety and quality. However, their expectations have increased as a result of cheap but reliable imports from Japan and the service-orientated culture associated with the United States. Before the increase in the car market of the Japanese and German cars with their reputation for reliability and service, British car owners were prepared to tolerate Monday morning and Friday afternoon cars which broke down with monotonous regularity. Now they have voted with their ignition keys. The same applies for service. Consumers expect this to be polite, informed and efficient. The great British past time of queuing is no longer tolerated. Businesses which in all other sense provide a good quality service can lose market share if they cannot find an effective way to reduce the length of queues.

With the growth of the consumer movement people are far more aware of their rights and have the confidence to insist upon them. Bank managers have been forced to refocus their attitudes to customers. They are no longer in a position to demand sub-servience from the customer but must seek to win business in a highly-competitive sector. People do exercise their rights with regard to inferior goods and services. Customer-orientated organizations such as Virgin place such a high priority on dealing with complaints that the chief executive sees every single one and ensures that it is followed up.

Organizations increasingly ask themselves are they number one or two in any given field? If they are not many are pulling out and subcontracting to others who are.

4

Customers wanting more choice

Customers expect more choice as our supermarket shelves testify. The comfortable days of long uninterrupted production runs are gone for many. Instead, manufacturers need to juggle switching from one short run to another. Production facilities and staff need to be more flexible. This tends to require more competent, better trained operatives. It also means extending your product range by forming alliances with other organizations and badging their products.

Production facilities and staff need to be more flexible.

Political change

The post-war years have seen phenomenal social and political change. The days of an easy run in Commonwealth markets are over. Sentiment has given over to commercial sense.

The strengthening and expansion of the European Union will lead to more specialization. Multinationals will continue to concentrate their production in fewer plants. This will mean that they will have just a marketing presence in some countries, with manufacturing carried out in a few super plants elsewhere.

The fall of the iron curtain has led to the transfer of many production lines. Investors are attracted by low wages and a high level of education. The Czech Republic has a long manufacturing tradition and is receiving a large amount of German investment. Over the next five years, East European exports will start having a big impact in our own industries.

We have also seen the emergence of China as a force in world trade. Who would have thought that the humble supermarket plastic bag may have come all the way from China? British Polythene are shifting half their production from Telford, Shropshire to Xinhui, Southern China. A growing range of industries will feel the impact of China's vast pool of cheap labour and commercial acumen.

5

The threat of the new

Unfortunately, you don't just have to worry about competition from existing players in your particular field, but the innovators who transfer successful business models to new industries. The marketplace already has a number of walking wounded whose businesses have been radically affected by the introduction of new models for example:

Direct Line which sells car and house insurance directly over the phone to customers has significantly changed the insurance market by cutting out the middleman and reducing costs. Some of the traditional insurance companies are beginning to follow suit. Direct Line is likely to shake up the mortgage market by offering low cost products over the telephone. Virgin Direct are starting to do this for stock exchange investments, using the same approach.

The spread of mail order from areas such as clothing to those as varied as books and computers. Computers lost their mystique and became virtually identical, reliable boxes. Sales staff and their expensive high street premises became more of an unnecessary overhead. How did they add value to the customer?

This is when mail order companies moved in and offered cheaper products. Is it too late to save the last ye olde computer shoppe?

Party plan selling which was once confined to the selling of plastic boxes (Tupperware) or cosmetics (Avon) has extended into shoes, books, jewellery, plants etc.

In all these examples, marketing concepts which are not unique in themselves, but new to that industry have resulted in significant loss of market share to those marketing in more traditional ways. The common feature is the stripping out of overhead costs which mean more attractive prices and robust IT systems which facilitate distribution to individuals.

Shorter product life-cycles

Consumers have bought into the marketing person's dream that fashions extend far beyond clothes to consumer durables of all types and to leisure activities. There is a real premium in being first in the marketplace be it for a revolutionary new product or a seductive variation or add-on which consumers feel they are unable to live without. This means that organizations need to speed up the design process. This can involve designers, production and marketing staff working together in project teams. Computers can be used intensively so that designers can see how their work fits in with each other. They can tackle different aspects at the same time, rather than wait for one to finish their work.

So what will this mean to your organization?

Your organization's survival will become increasingly threatened. The realistic view is that most organizations fail, it is just a question of when. They could survive for a few years or a few hundred years. Look at Lloyd's and Barings. So what can you do to postpone the evil day? You will have to get much closer to your customers to find out what they really want and what are your products' minor niggles. Customer surveys and customer complaints will have to be taken much more seriously. This will include encouraging customers to complain if they are dissatisfied, before they desert you for a competitor. How well equipped is your organization to do this?

Innovation is vital. What does your organization do to encourage it? How does it involve staff in solving problems and working out future strategy?

Faster decision making is also crucial. How can your organization improve? Many organizations have removed tiers of management to speed decision making and to reduce costs. Computer systems can provide information for top management rather than middle managers. Empowered front-line staff make more decisions themselves and need fewer managers. Where is your organization on this continuum?

This hopefully is beginning to raise your anxiety on a number of levels. Will your organization survive because it is currently doing a very good ostrich impersonation? Will you survive the measures your organization is taking to improve its chances for its own continuation? You need to be sufficiently disturbed by this to be galvanized into acting now. Winning at change must become your number one priority. In delayered, downsized organizations there is space for winners only.

Checklist of what your organization can do:

- continuously improve products and services

- become customer obsessed, carry out regular surveys

- be more innovative

- increase the international appeal of products

- sell knowledge and production equipment to emerging economies

- make faster decisions

- delayer

- organize production more flexibly

- concentrate on what it is really good at

- make more alliances

- place greater emphasis on learning

- improve the quality, flexibility and training of production staff.

So what can you do?

Flatter organizations and empowered staff are changing the role for the fewer surviving managers. They are increasingly used to coach staff. You will begin to find the power you expected by virtue of your position in the hierarchy being eroded by those who have the knowledge and skills needed to deliver change. Expert power is beginning to replace position power. This places a premium on having a facilitative style and good influencing skills. It means letting your staff learn through making some non-fatal mistakes. This will be very difficult, especially as you might think you know the 'answer'. One of the things you will need to teach them is how to learn and become self-sufficient. Remember few people get it right first time. If you help them too much you will teach them to become dependent on others. One of the things you may have to learn is to 'let go'.

People currently tend to work in cosy functional enclaves where they enjoy common language skills, experiences and mindsets. How many of us have referred to the typical accountant or the caring sharing personnel manager. To address the issues of change effectively projects need to be established across functional boundaries. This will require good teamworking skills. Like in a sports team you will need to know what the other member of the team can contribute as well as performing well yourself. How good are you at teamworking?

Could you further your career by learning a foreign language? If you are planning a career move, would learning a language be attractive to multinationals? How comfortable are you with coping with foreign customs? Would you use chop sticks in Asian restaurants? If not, why not? Are you frightened of making a fool of yourself? This would be a serious handicap to you as learning often involves you making mistakes. We forget that children don't learn to walk first time so why should we expect to learn much more complicated skills and get them right first time?

Can you put yourself in the position of your customers? We are all customers outside the workplace but do not take our experiences or frame of reference into the working environment in order to understand our own customers. This requires you to be open in your dealings with people be they customers, colleagues or junior staff. Do you seek out the truth even though it demonstrates you are wrong? Do you ask for feedback? If you get it, do you ignore it?

In times of anxiety people tend to over rely on courses of action that have worked in the past but are now demonstrably failing. They lose their perspective and the ability to recognize that their solution is part of the problem. You will need to recognize when it is time not to work harder but to work more creatively.

What do you do to encourage innovation? Do you overdo the head down and clear your desk routine? What if you spent half an hour a week thinking? It takes time to become really creative.

9

With such rapid change, knowledge can fast become obsolete. What are you doing to keep up-to-date? Do you go to conferences? Read books and articles? Belong to professional societies? Have you thought of raising your profile through writing articles? This can lead to invitations to speak at conferences. Getting your name about might lead to job offers or at least improve your curriculum vitae. This is particularly important as there may be fewer opportunities for promotion within your own organization.

Assess your skills and knowledge base

Now is the time to make the first assessment of how big a task you have before you gear yourself up to being a manager of tomorrow. Complete the table below truthfully and quickly. Do not spend a lot of time analyzing the questions and your responses to them. If you think you may not be able to be objective, check your answers with a friend or colleague. Do not be worried if your score is a low one because this book is aimed at improving your skills and knowledge in all these areas. Later in the book you will have the opportunity to assess your competencies in more detail.

Competencies and activities	Score				
	very good 5	good 4	average 3	poor 2	very poor 1
How good are you at coaching?					
How good are you at influencing others?					
How good are you at team working?					
How good are you at project management?					
	10+	9–6	5–4	3–2	1–0
How many business books do you read a year?					
How often do you go to conferences, professional societies etc. a year?					
	In last year	1 year ago	2 years ago	3 years ago	4+ years
Have you learnt any new knowledge or skills eg a foreign language or swimming?					
When was the last new idea of yours accepted and implemented by your organization?					
Total					

10

Scoring guide

	Points scored per question	Overall total
Very good	5	36–40
Good	4	30–35
Average	3	25–29
Poor	2	20–24
Very poor	1	19 and under

It is very difficult to accept that your skills which were once highly regarded might now be viewed as outmoded and inappropriate.

2
...

Can you manage in the whirlpool?

Acknowledging your own feelings · the end of traditional careers · the rise of do-it-yourself careers · loss of control over empowered staff · a poisoned working atmosphere · the sense of loss and the bereavement process

How to continue your personal success
■ ■ ■

How you are feeling right now depends on why you bought this book in the first place. Are you already feeling the pain and anxiety of your organization launching into major corporate surgery? Or are you at the stage of waking in the hours of darkness and thinking those thoughts that you would not dare to admit during daylight? It is not happening now in your organization but the signs are there. On the other hand, you might be riding high in an extremely successful organization but you like to stay ahead of the game. To continue your winning streak, you realize that you need to anticipate the future in order to influence its direction rather than become its victim. Whatever your motivations are, the essential first step to winning at work is to truly admit how you feel about its impact on your life.

Acknowledging your own feelings

As part of the British culture we are taught from an early age not to show our feelings. Do you remember when you were a child being told not to cry when you had really hurt yourself or were very frightened? Our immediate reaction was to feel that our pain and fear were being denied and that we should seek to deny them ourselves. It is not surprising therefore that many of us have difficulty in acknowledging our fear of the unknown. This is particularly true of men who are frequently told as little boys to be brave and not cry. Girls are not socialized in the same way. They are not forced to subdue the more feminine side of their personality until they progress up the corporate ladder and are expected to behave like honoury men.

Organization change

Organizations will never be the same again. They will require fewer people of a different type. Charles Handy, in his book 'The Age of Unreason'[1] predicted that jobs in organizations for the

[1] Century Hutchinson Ltd (1989)

next generations are only going to occupy 50,000 hours (equal to about 25 years) instead of 100,000 hours that they have done previously. This means shorter working lives within organizations not more leisure time. This thought frightens the hell out of most people because what else will they do? In the twentieth century most of us, but particularly men have invested all in our jobs or 'careers'. We have looked to them for so many things – interest, job satisfaction, social interaction, money, security and social status. Now confronting downsizing delayering, restructuring, re-engineering in every industry and all over the shrinking public sector, we are having to cope with the loss of the career concept. Robin Linnear, partner at KPMG Career Consultancy Services comments, 'there is no such thing as a career path anymore. It is crazy paving and you have to lay it yourself.'[1] The challenge for you is what are you going to put in place of the paternalistic employer who in exchange for hard work, loyalty and commitment gave you security and a long-term career?

15

The end of traditional careers

You also need to confront what losing your job or that promotion you were expecting really would mean to you. Would it just be concerns around loss of current and future income or would it be far more profound? Is your feeling of self worth intrinsically tied in with you career? If so, it would follow that losing your job or your next promotion would somehow make you a less worthy person? We are all human and we should feel valued for being who we are. However, if you only feel valued if you are being promoted, this can be a great motivator. What happens when this stops?

In Western society people are rewarded with highly visible badges for their success. This includes expensive cars, plush offices, large desks, expense accounts and reserved parking spaces. In fact we have turned this into such an art form that people use the level of trappings to judge the status of others. This therefore highlights any decrease in status because the loss of them is equally apparent, not only to the individual but all around them.

[1] *Management Today*, February 1995, Simon Caulkin 'Take your Partners'.

Another equally painful loss is writing off past investment in your career. This could cover all manner of things from working long hours, sacrificing time with friends and family to spending personal time studying for required qualifications, accepting overseas assignments in unappealing locations. For some women this could include postponing having a family until it was too late. This would have seemed worthwhile if it had resulted in reaching the pinnacle to which you aspired, but how do you feel now that the rules have been changed?

Obsolescence is a further obstacle to overcome. It is very difficult to accept that your skills which were once highly regarded might now be viewed as outmoded and inappropriate. The familiar management style of command and control that you probably practise instinctively is now being replaced by coaching, facilitating and teambuilding skills. Does this excite or terrify you? It requires the delegation of responsibility rather than tasks that could leave you feeling that you have given away power and therefore lost control. It is very hard for you if you have been weaned on command and control to let go to allow seeds to germinate and grow with gentle nurturing and support.

A poisoned working atmosphere

When organizations are confronting significant organizational change the working atmosphere begins to change. Initially these changes can appear minor. Collectively they have the effect of transforming the feelings of camaraderie, trust and loyalty into those of intrigue, backstabbing, gossip and competing to be favourite. Do you respond to these feelings by working longer hours, wanting to be first in in the morning and the last to leave at night? Do you feel people are talking behind your back? The problem with this change in atmosphere is that it creeps slowly like poisonous gas – it is very difficult to detect until it is choking you. You cannot afford to ignore these symptoms. However, you also must not dissipate your time and effort by succumbing to them. Your energy should be channelled positively into your own survival plan.

You could be sitting there smugly now thinking this is all very distressing but if this happens in my company I will look around and find another organization that is not undergoing such turmoil. There I will be able to continue safely in my current mindset and my career can progress unimpeded by change. This will not work. It is like being a non swimmer in the swimming pool. You can probably move from the hand rail to the rubber ring and onto a float. All these aids will prevent you from drowning. However, you will never be able to survive in the tidal wave that breaks over the side of the swimming pool until you can swim in the deep end. You need to teach yourself the equivalent skills to swimming so that you can throw away your buoyancy aids and swim in whichever organizational ocean appeals to you.

The sense of loss and the bereavement process

All these losses add up to a significant bereavement that could cause a similar amount of personal distress as the loss of a loved one. An understanding of the stages experienced during bereavement will give you an idea of what to expect and help you to plan how to overcome them. It is essential that you actually allow yourself to experience all of these stages and do not use up precious resources by resisting them. They must be acknowledged, expressed and worked through.

The first is that of **shock**. You are told one of these sorts of things:

> *'You have not got that promotion'.*
> *'Your level of the organization is being delayered'* .
> *'Your management style is no longer appropriate'.*
> *'We are doing things differently around here from now on'.*
> *'Management perks are to be abolished'.*
> *'All information is to be shared with everyone'.*

You do not know what has hit you. You are paralyzed. Either it was totally unexpected or else the realization of your worst fears.

It can't happen to me? You are now entering the world of **denial**. You live in the make believe land that somehow everything will be all right again – your organization will turn around or your department will not be affected or somehow you will come out of it completely unscathed.

Anger comes as the gross sense of injustice manifests itself. The anger can be directed outwards towards other people. You may feel really angry at your boss, the board or the holding company. They are to blame. This anger could be directed towards colleagues and that you are going to survive at the cost of others if necessary. This could go as far as contributing towards their downfall. On the other hand the anger can be directed at the invisible force, why did it have to happen to me? There is no way out when **depression** strikes. Everything feels leaden and hopeless. Like shock and denial, depression is a passive state when you are at your most vulnerable.

Realization takes place when you can no longer delude yourself that change will go away. This can take place slowly for those who gradually piece together the jigsaw of minor change that collectively means that things will never be the same again. For others, the realization smacks them in between the eyes by the sudden departure of a colleague or worse still, being asked to clear their own desk.

Again it must be emphasized that you must acknowledge your feelings otherwise you could become stuck in one of these stages and unconsciously sabotage your own effort at recovery. We have all experienced the manager who talks about the way things used to be. Their frame of reference is to things that happened in the past, not how different things will need to be in the future. One of the greatest risks of being stuck in the past is not seeing the opportunities around you for the taking. If you are felt to be a relic of the past you will not be considered as a prime candidate for the navigator of organizational change. There is not much call for archivists in the organizations of the future.

Energy found in the anger phase can be used positively to motivate you to succeed in spite of what you feel has been done to you. It is more productive to channel your energies in constructive pursuits rather than destructive ones around getting even or back at people.

Of course you may not be threatened just yet, but most people know someone who has been. Try to share some of their experiences because this could allow you to participate in some anticipatory grieving that will put you in much better shape for when it happens to you.

We have tended to emphasize the negative aspects of this experience but there are some overwhelmingly positive ones. You will never be complacent about success again. It is an obvious, simple lesson but it cannot be fully appreciated second-hand. You must experience the feelings to ensure that you will be ready for change when it next comes your way and make the most of the opportunities it brings.

Do not feel that you will have come through unscathed because you have survived. Survivors from major disasters have been known to be consumed by guilt. This is also true in the workplace. If many colleagues and subordinates or just one or two have lost their jobs you will feel guilty even though you did not particularly like them or feel that they were good at their job.

19

Whilst you are going through this process you will need support. Do not automatically view colleagues, clients, associates as members of that support group. Select a safe circle of friends outside work to talk about your feelings. Now is not the time to wear your heart on your sleeve. You want to take only the positive, creative, innovative you to work. Make use of independent counsellors and outplacement facilities

Light appears between the dark clouds when **resolution** appears. Life is perceived to go on beyond this event. It is only when you reach this point that you can start to consider new strategies and beginnings.

The sooner you allow yourself to feel the pain the sooner it will pass. If you postpone the healing process, grief can return months or even years later and haunt you. When you are vulnerable, look after your health, rest and exercise in moderation. At the very end of the process, try to remember the good times.

Again it must be emphasized that you must acknowledge your feelings otherwise you could become stuck in one of these stages or unconsciously sabotage your own efforts at recovery. You should not live in the past but acknowledge it and then move on. Each person can experience the sequence differently or indeed move back and forward between the stages. Do not be alarmed if this happens to you. Just accept that this is part of the process and that you will move forward.

This section should be reread when you are bringing about change so that you can deal with people sensitively and effectively as you can tune into their feelings.

To help you assess the ways that you are feeling at the moment complete as honestly as you can the table below. This table shows a continuum and you should score where you currently think you are. If you are not sure how aware you are of your feelings, ask a close friend to help you, based on their observation of your behaviour. Do not worry if most of your feelings are negative at the moment, ie you have a low score. You should score yourself again at the end of the book and at regular intervals as you unfold your action plan.

From	1	2	3	4	5	To
threatened						secure
confused						clear
trapped						empowered
deskilled						enabled
angry						content
frustrated						opportunistic
humiliated						praised
undervalued						valued
too busy						doing the right things well
under pressure						meeting deadlines
aimless						focused
Total						

Scoring guide

Points scored overall

Very negative	under 18
Negative	19–30
Fairly positive	31–40
Positive	41+

You may now be feeling very depressed because your score has shown that you are in a very negative frame of mind. Or you may have scored high and feel ready for any changes that confront you. But how confident are you? Wouldn't you really like to know how you can become the sort of person who not only copes well with change, but positively blossoms with the opportunities that change puts up for grabs? We want to show you how to become a change winner. We will reveal the profile of these winning people to you. Not so that you can try to clone yourself but so you begin to understand what makes them so successful in change situations. You can then decide for yourself those competencies you wish to acquire and those approaches and behaviours that you would wish to incorporate into your own repertoire.

The rise of do-it-yourself careers

A change winner is someone who:

- has a strong self-image
- possesses a high level of self-knowledge
- is flexible
- looks for feedback
- has good interpersonal skills
- looks beyond the short term
- sees life as a learning opportunity
- can take calculated risks
- sees feedback where others see mistakes and failures
- focuses internally for security and not externally

■ does not strongly seek approval from others.

They are also:

■ customer-focused

■ eager to empower staff.

This profile has been drawn up from ours and others' observations of both successful and unsuccessful responses to change. We have learnt as much if not more from the failures than from the success. Position in the hierarchy nor success in the past are clear indicators that someone will be a change winner. More junior managers often fit the profile more easily than their bosses who have more to lose. Successful people in the past may be more inclined to repeat a formula that previously led to success and be less willing to take risks in trying out untried approaches.

22

Are you ready to embark on this journey that could fundamentally change your approach to the rest of your career? This exploration could sever the link that most of us have between success in our career and organizations. This does not mean that you will not continue to work for an organization if that is where you can see opportunities for personal development. What it does mean is that your security and your career plan will be focused entirely on you and your ability to change, adapt and learn from the opportunities available. It may not be an easy journey. There may be some spectacular views from the peaks of high achievement and self-realization but also some dismal valleys. However, you will never be the victim of corporate mass manipulation again. Those of us who are making this journey, continue to work with and for organizations but we know that our success is totally in our own hands and only we can take it away from ourselves.

So what maps are we offering you for this journey? You will find out more about yourself – your learning style, values, personality profile, etc. in chapters 3 and 4. This will give you an idea of how close you are to the change winner's profile. It will highlight areas on which you may like to concentrate. We explore the latest management approaches in chapter 5 to save you reading the numerous books, articles and conference write-ups. We then ask you to look at the reality in your own organization currently and in the future so that you can customize the approach to change to meet your particular situation. This is followed up by hints and practical methods for acquiring the skills for mastering change and for influencing its direction. Action plans are included close to the end to ensure that you don't just consider that this could simply be a very interesting journey, but that you actually plan your route, select your mode of transport and then do it.

23

Some people are discouraged from realizing their learning potential by social pressures.

3
■ ■ ■

Can you meet the challenge?

What is learning? · how do you learn? · can you receive feedback? · are you prepared to experiment? · what level of risk can you cope with?

Attitudes to learning

■ ■ ■

In the past, it was thought learning knowledge took place in school and for some also in further education. Then it was a matter of acquiring practical skills at work at the beginning of a career, and with a bit of luck, that was it. How things have changed. Global competition is reducing the shelf life of products and the knowledge and skills that lie behind them. The pace of change can be frightening. Knowledge that was leading edge at one minute can become obsolete the next. Therefore it is the capacity to learn rather than knowledge that is the key. Successful organizations have to learn, adapt and change continuously as do the individuals within them. This is echoed in the rapid growth of knowledge workers. It is affecting all levels of organizations. Thinking workers out perform obedient ones who depend on instructions from an army of supervisors. It is knowledge rather than capital that provides the edge to beat the competition. The objective is to work smarter not harder to use Drucker's words. Organizations need to go beyond maintenance learning of the known and reoccurring through problem-solving techniques. They need to prepare for major discontinuity through innovative learning that anticipates the future. This requires the capability to analyze information, speculate, imagine and discuss, rather than passively reacting to change.

Learning can be unthreatening when it adds to our existing skills and knowledge. Building on the foundations of earlier generations can be very satisfying. However, sometimes it is necessary to demolish their proud monuments before the foundations of new can be laid. Many years of hard work and imagination are bulldozed on to the waste tip of knowledge. This is because some of the new approaches and knowledge contradicts what went before. You may be required to unlearn what you hold dear. This is the hardest learning of all. It can cause you feelings of pain and of loss when your handiwork is turned into rubble.

Our attitudes to learning are very deep rooted as they touch on how we feel about ourselves and our identity. This can date back our school days when a teacher might have said you are poor at _____ (fill in whatever applies to you). This can result in a feeling of failure and giving up on that subject entirely. We may take this negative mindset wherever we go in life. It can be a serious handicap as school subjects support a range of learning styles such as skilful questioning, observation, analysis, structuring information into meaningful frameworks, role playing and experimentation. The more of these that we have at our disposal, the easier it is to learn later in life. However, school learning tends to undervalue unstructured and action based learning. This explains why some of those who excel at such approaches can be highly successful at work yet have been regarded as failures at school.

Are you lucky enough to have had a teacher who inspired you and boosted your confidence? If you had, it will be much easier for you to find mentors and role models whenever you need them. It will also make it easier for you to support and encourage the learning of others. Tell them that they are good at things when they get it right. In that way they will begin to incorporate success at the task into their identity. When someone makes a mistake, never say they are wrong, rather that there is an error in their work. Ask them what the mistake is and what they would do instead, rather than giving them the correct answer. This will avoid discouraging them into believing that they are failures.

27

Some people are discouraged from realizing their learning potential by social pressures. Class, ethnic, religious and gender expectations interact with each other to influence our choice of what we learn and how far we are willing to take it. It used to be thought perfectly normal for girls to do less well at 'boys' subjects such as mathematics and science. Now girls out perform boys in these subjects as well. No doubt it will take time before employers respond to these changes and employ more women in engineering and technical jobs. There are many other examples of social expectations influencing our willingness to learn. Some older managers do not want to get to grips with computers as they associate them with lower status roles such as that of secretaries. Some women are held back by their own low career expectations and others by passive, unassertive behaviour. This is also true for a smaller group of men. Another counterproductive behaviour, particularly in teamworking is aggression. Both can be tackled by assertiveness training courses. These are often tailored to meet the needs of a specific group.

The learning process
■ ■ ■

The stages of learning

Learning something completely new can be an uncomfortable journey. It starts out with blissful ignorance about what exactly we need to learn and how long it will take us to master it. The next stage is very uncomfortable: knowing just how little you know. If this feeling overwhelms you, it is very easy to give up. This is where having real staying power can make all the difference. The reward for perseverance is usually a tolerable level of competence. This might feel slightly awkward at first, rather like just having passed a driving test. Your head is full of endless chatter, spelling out each action in great detail. Gradually and without realizing it, you seem to do things automatically and can no longer recall the details of how one drives. The stages that learners typically go through are:

- unconscious incompetence

- conscious incompetence

- conscious competence

- unconscious competence

Perceptual preferences

Have you noticed how some people say things *look good*, others say they *sound fine* and for some it just *feels right*? What this tells you is that people perceive things visually, auditorally and kinaesthetically. Most of you will have strong preferences in how you process experiences and information. What is yours? The most powerful learning combines all three elements. Picture what you want, tell yourself how much you want it and feel what it would be like to succeed. Remember these differences when you are working with others. Mirror the other person's preferences. Visual people can quickly see what you mean when you draw a diagram or paint a picture with words. Catch the mood of feeling people before getting involved in the detail. Show patience if they occasionally pause in the middle of a conversation or veer off a logical path. Auditory people like to talk things through, so help them do so. When relating to a group, combine all three elements as your audience is likely to be made up of each type. This technique is used in some of the checklists below.

The learning cycle

There are a number of different learning cycles but the one we have found most useful is Kolb's[1]. It involves a sequence of:

- **concrete experience** – learning from feeling

- **reflective observation** – learning by watching and listening

- **abstract conceptualization** – learning by thinking

- **active experimentation** – learning by doing.

Each person's learning style is a combination of the four basic styles. Most people have one or more styles that they are more comfortable with. This may well distort their ability to learn and also tend to pull them towards particular phases of the learning cycle. Beware you do not purely use those styles with which you feel most at home because you could be missing vital learning opportunities.

How to improve your learning

Some of the learning strategies below will be very familiar to you, while you may not be in tune with others. Nevertheless, the more of them you can use, the easier it will be for you to learn.

[1] David Kolb *Learning Style Inventory*, McBer and Company 1985.

Cultural fit

Do you know of people who go on courses, who can talk about what they have learnt, but fail to put it into practice? This might be managers who went on an empowerment course. They might think it a great idea until they realize the consequences for themselves. This is no more than token learning. In other cases learners just back from a course are not given the time or the scope to put into practice what they have learnt. They then start to forget and lose confidence so the learning does not stick. Some organizations take this lack of payback from training as an excuse to cut back on training. However, what is needed is a learning culture that integrates training and work more closely together.

Keep your eye on the prize

Inspirational leaders use their imagination to paint vivid pictures of the fruits of success and sense of fulfilment that they will bring. This gives them and their followers the necessary hope and enthusiasm that along with perseverance will help overcome the challenges of learning. Imagination will also help you to run through the consequences of different actions in your mind. This will make it easier to explore a wider range of options before making a decision. Imagination will help you devise radical solutions that break with the past. Would you like to be more imaginative? The secret is to indulge your thoughts and follow them where they go. Sometimes the direction lacks logic. Wait for your journey to come to its natural end before evaluating the results. To give the momentum to succeed create your own vision by going through the steps below.

- what are the gains to you once you have achieved your learning goals?

- what would it feel like when you have achieved them?

- what would you hear others say to you and what did you tell yourself?

- what does this look like in your mind's eye?

Persevere

Learning can be unsettling and this may require staying power to overcome. You need to be able to call on this resource when you need it to succeed. Young children have this quality in abundance. There are not many recorded cases of children refusing to learn to walk because they fell over the first few times they tried it!

■ can you think back to a time when you showed perseverance and were successful?

■ what did it feel like?

■ what did you hear others say to you and what did you tell yourself?

■ what does this look like in your mind's eye?

Recruit supporters

You can speed up the learning process by having role models. These are people who have the skill or behaviour you wish to emulate. You can ask yourself what would they do or say in a particular situation. You then compare it with your own intentions to increase your range of options. You can even have a couple of role models with contrasting styles to extend the choice available to you. The real benefit of a role model is when you feel you are stuck, trying out what they would do would give you a way forward. Once you have mastered their script, you will have the confidence and capability to write your own.

■ who has the skills and competencies that you want to acquire?

■ how can you build up your knowledge bank of what they do by seeing and hearing them in action more often?

Mentors are usually very experienced practitioners who are not directly involved in the problems for which you seek guidance. Their role is to help you clarify your thinking so that you ask the right questions rather than give you answers. Some organizations have a formal network of mentors. However, there is nothing to stop you asking someone whom you respect for occasional advice. You will be surprised how often people are flattered when they are asked for help. Therefore do not feel put off to approach someone for advice if you have not done it before.

- choose an experienced player to approach who does not have a direct stake in the problem you are likely to encounter

- when are they most likely to respond favourably to your approach?

Get stuck in

Learning through action can be very effective. Learning sets can provide a safe environment to get your hands on experience, so do not hold back.

Experiment

For young children learning, playing and fun are rolled up together. The experience of school can make learning feel dry and boring. As adults we can recapture that sense of fun by going abroad, eating new food and trying out new experiences. Children try out everything before they stick with some new learning. This is a useful approach for the world of work as there is usually more than one right answer. In a rapidly changing world, the more options you have up your sleeve the better. Only after having explored the many different ways of doing things should you use the adult skill of assessment. Designers and some research staff are very experienced experimenters.

- observe how children play and learn

- experiment with food and try a complete new type of cuisine. Eat with chop sticks, if you have never done so

- experience new forms of entertainment such as opera, a classical concert, jazz club or art gallery.

- try out as many different ways of doing things as possible before settling for a preferred approach.

Take risks

Young children are some of the fastest learners. They achieve this by not concerning themselves with what others think of their efforts. Stage fright is something that is learnt later in life. People who are successful in other settings can freeze when the spotlight is turned on them. Those who have once experienced defeat snatched from the jaws of victory may be particularly prone to this feeling. They fear they might repeat their mistakes. Some people prefer to go through life concealing their ignorance rather than admitting that they do not know something. They live in fear of being caught out and when this happens they feel mortified. If you find risk taking difficult, go back to the stage of eyeing up the prize. Concentrate on thinking about succeeding at what you are doing. What you think will happen often will, especially if your head is cluttered with negative thoughts. Role playing is a very useful way to try out new behaviours and skills in a safe setting. Asking for feedback can be a useful way to learn. Yet some ignore it as it carries with it the risk that it may be negative. The following questions offer other ways to increase risk taking.

33

- What is the worst that can happen to you if you cannot do something or if you fail in the attempt?

- what would help you make light of such situations? Can you think of someone else who would have made a joke about it?

- what is the safest setting for you to learn?

- think of a time when you were successful at taking risks.

- what does it look like in your mind's eye?

- what did other people say and what did you tell yourself?

- what did it feel like?

- volunteer to be the first person to have a go in a training setting – everyone else will admire your courage and you will be setting the standard for the other learners.

Learn from your own experience

Formal education tends to under value practical experience. Yet this can be a great asset when faced with new learning. Trial and error can show us what works, when and under what conditions. In addition, experience can give us confidence by recalling an occasion when we have tackled something similar successfully. However, many of us are too narrow and literal when we search our memories. This makes learning feel like an unsettling voyage into the unknown. Experience can be used as a stick to beat one-self by those who spend more time and effort recalling failure than reflecting on success. It is important to learn the lessons and then move on. See what others call failure as merely feedback.

Think of the successful experience closest to the learning you wish to undertake.

■ what did it feel like?

■ what did you hear others say to you and what did you tell yourself?

■ what does this look like in your mind's eye?

Be structured and systematic

Comparing and contrasting actions and strategies and placing them in a framework is invaluable when learning complicated subjects. It also helps to integrate new learning with existing knowledge. This underpins the competencies of planning change and project management. Planners and researchers tend to have these qualities in abundance. One way to enhance your capabilities is to go on a project management training course. This has the further attraction of becoming an increasingly sought after skill. You can also:

■ read the same story in two very different newspapers.
  – what are the similarities and differences and how do they relate to their political views? Decide beforehand on some of the measures you are going to use.

■ compare your organization with a very different type of one and assess their strengths and weaknesses.

     – what are the differences and similarities and what
     might lie behind them?

■ ask 'why' five times when analyzing a problem until you
   reach the root cause.

Be intuitive

It is not possible to break all learning down into small, measurable steps. Some learning comes to you in flash, if you are willing to acknowledge it. This is familiar to those people who have gut feelings about something. They are often open to their feelings and situations without over analyzing them. The following will help you become more intuitive:

■ when dealing with a problem, take note of your first
   answer

■ consider it carefully and remember it for future reference.

35

Types of behaviour and learning preferences
■ ■ ■

Have you noticed how people confronted with the same problem can behave quite differently? Some dive in straight away and get to grips with the task in hand. Others want to deal with the people issues first. The more analytical might want to gather more information before selecting a preferred option and then coming up with an action plan. Each type of approach has its strengths and weaknesses. It is important to have a mix of as many of them as you can when selecting a team. Some organizations and functions are more likely to attract certain types than others. Action people and technocrats are found in large numbers where managing processes is critical such as a chemical plant or steel works. Personnel is likely to have a large number of diplomats. Some people fit a particular category very tightly. However, others combine aspects of a couple of them. Perhaps with one more dominant than the other.

People differ not only in the way they respond to situations but how they learn. By understanding these differences you will feel more comfortable when dealing with people different from you. This is important to you as supporting the learning of others is a key managerial responsibility. The links between types of people and how they learn are set out below. It should be pointed out that the relationship is close but not absolute, so expect a few exceptions. Which descriptions in the section below fits you best?

Action people

They make the best fire-fighters as they like to take charge of emergencies. They are quick and decisive and have a strong task orientation. They are very effective in command and control organizations. An early patron of action people was Alexander the Great. When confronted with the Gordian knot that no one was able to unravel, he cut it with his sword. Not surprisingly such people do not have well-developed fire prevention skills. Diplomacy is not a strong point either. When faced with a crisis they risk becoming so obsessed with activity that they lose sight of the desired outcome. As they hate resting on their shovels they can be great hole diggers.

Throwing action people a challenge is a great way to energize this type of learner. They like to learn by walking about and seeing things in practice. They value case studies and practical tips. They take a strong dislike to theoretical approaches and complicated explanations.

Diplomats

They want to feel comfortable with the other people involved in doing a task before getting on with it. They work energetically to create and maintain harmony and are willing to pay a high price to avoid conflict. They attach more value on group success than on individual gains. They add the human touch and are the heart and soul of a working group. Their low key approach means that their contribution can go undervalued. On leaving, their loss is deeply felt and unless there is another diplomat in the group, its character takes on a colder task orientated feel.

They prefer to learn in supportive settings where there is a high degree of co-operation. They want the company of people with whom they can relate closely. Learning needs to be relevant to human needs and aspirations, rather than being an end in itself. Role models and mentors whose personal qualities they respect can be a great influence on them. Other people are keen to select diplomats as mentors because they are so approachable. Diplomats tend to dislike theoretical and formal approaches to learning.

Diplomats can also make good networkers. They can seem to know everything that is going on and everyone who matters. They scan the external environment and like to learn from other organizations and are good at importing ideas.

Opportunists

They are risk takers who like wheeling and dealing. They focus on the here and now. Their feel for people means that they have a good sense of what they want and they can use this to manipulate the situation to their benefit. They enjoy as much autonomy as they can get and tend to rebel against rules and formal structures. The marketing and sales environments provide happy homes for people with such an entrepreneurial style.

Their learning style is flexible and pragmatic. They can learn from people, experience or any other source if the mood takes them.

Technocrats

They take an analytical perspective and like to compare and contrast ideas and approaches. They take time to make decisions because they want to fit together all the pieces of the jigsaw puzzle first.

Their planning and organization skills are of a high order. As perfectionists they are critical of their own efforts and those of others. Situations that require diplomacy, flexibility and decisiveness can be troublesome to them.

When it comes to learning, they want to be convinced that the underlying thinking is robust, with clear aims and objectives before they become involved. Their learning is methodical and they like generating hypotheses, developing suitable tests and evaluating the results. They dislike learning that is anecdotal, lacking in structure and coherence.

Strategists

They are innovators who can foresee long-term possibilities. They can capture the imagination of others and give them the energy to move forward. Their flexibility and mental agility means that they can unravel complexity. Moving from the individual group to corporate level is done with ease and elegance. They have insight into themselves and others so they can see an issue from all angles. As they feel they do not have all the answers, they are keen to involve others. They can build strong teams with complementary skills. They can build powerful coalitions as they look for win-win solutions. They are very skilled managers of organizational change. They use learning to achieve an overarching ambition that fits into the bigger picture, and they are keen to learn from whatever source.

Gurus

They are of the world but are not part of it. They transcend the detail to see the underlying principles and fundamental values. They are masters of ideas and thoughts and are an inspiration to others. They learn from the realms of knowledge and experience. Their strength lies in knowing the right questions and encouraging the exploration of others. They are less suited to situations that require a quick response or detailed, practical application.

Bon voyage
■ ■ ■

Action people can be of great value when their work supports the overall direction of change. However, they can lack the reflective qualities required to come up with new approaches required by the changing environment. The diplomats may feel the human costs of change very deeply and this may undermine their effectiveness. Opportunists would be flexible enough to cope with change and would enjoy the lack of rules and procedures that are usually associated with such periods: risk taking and an entrepreneurial character is part of their style. However, they may lack the long-term vision to switch to new activities while the old ones still produce a return. Technocrats may have a vitally important knowledge base but can lack the flexibility to be comfortable with change. Gurus can act as guides to be called on when needed. Strategists have the long-term vision and adaptability to play a key role in change. This tends to be the preferred style of change winners. Nevertheless, they would understand each of the characteristics listed and value their use in the appropriate situation. However, they would be particularly keen to acquire those aspects they do not already have.

Further reading

Total Quality Learning, Building A Learning Organization, Ronnie Lessem, Blackwell (1994) – this chapter draws on several of the ideas and approaches from this book.

***R**ealization is the first step in personal development*

4

■ ■ ■

Assessing yourself

What is a change winner? · What are your underlying
prejudices? · How good are you at communicating? · What
is your preferred leadership style? · How good a
teamplayer are you? · Assessing risk · The Belbin team
types · Are you a change winner?

As businesses scramble to develop approaches that better suit today's fast changing environment they are beginning to scrutinize the success formulas and attributes of senior managers. A growing number have concluded that the intense, ambitious drive that has propelled many executives up the organizational ladder does not always work so well in the new, more participative cultures.

Robert Kaplan in his book *'Beyond Ambition'*[1] describes some of the limitations of the old style high-achieving executive as follows:

■ aversion to risk

■ roughshod treatment of subordinates and failure to delegate

■ coldness, aloofness, rigidity

■ a focus on empire building and self-aggrandisement

■ an inordinate concern with getting ahead and status symbols

■ an inability to distinguish between high and low priorities

■ over extending and burning out themselves or their people

■ an inflated sense of their own importance

■ an ability to distort reality to create a favourable impression

■ lack of integrity.

Whilst some of his observations are undoubtedly rather harsh there is no doubt that managers who excelled in high command and control environment find it difficult to adapt to the new evolving environment. Unfortunately while their limitations are only too visible to superiors, peers and subordinates, they are rarely recognized by the executives themselves.

You are probably saying right now that none of these things

[1] Jossey Bass Inc, San Francisco, (1991).

could possibly apply to you, but who are you fooling? In order to win in the constantly changing environment you must have a realistic assessment of yourself – your prejudices, your interpersonal skills, your leadership style, your preferred behavioural style, etc. Now comes the really difficult part, we are going to take you through a number of tests that will help you assess yourself.

What is a change winner
■ ■ ■

In chapter 2 we identified the profile of those people who win at change as:

- having a strong self image
- possessing a high level of self-knowledge
- being flexible
- looking for feedback
- having good interpersonal skills
- planning ahead
- seeing life as a learning opportunity
- taking calculated risks
- focusing internally for security
- customer-orientated
- a team player.

We want you to compare against this profile not so that you model yourself on it totally but so you can decide which competencies you already have and which you may wish to acquire to help you be successful in change situations.

Sir Len Peach in his article, 'Don't blame HR for the Company's Failure,'[1] referred to a recent survey into business leadership where 600 or so managers responded as follows:

[1] 'People Management', 29 June 1995.

43

- business leaders should be able to build effective teams, said 89 per cent, but only 47 per cent thought their CEO could

- business leaders should know how to listen, said 84 per cent, but only 47 per cent indicated that their CEO did

- CEOs should surround themselves with the right people, said 83 per cent, but only 42 per cent do.

You can see from these statistics that the reality within many organizations is that they have a great need for their change winners to emerge.

Please try and be honest with all the tests, because you will only be kidding yourself if you are not. If you cannot trust yourself, then check out your findings with a trusted friend or supporter.

Realization is the first step in personal development. An approach to change that looks at both behaviour and the underlying character that creates it is needed. The aim of these tests is not to indulge in a clean sweep of the inner self, but to give you a better sense of what is important and what you are about.

44

What are your underlying prejudices?
■ ■ ■

This first test is a very simple one to look at some of your underlying prejudices.

Try to give a true response to the following statements, rather than those you know to be politically correct. This will give you a rough idea of where you think you stand.

		Yes	No
1	I am always objective.	☐	☐
2	I try to approach all problems with a totally open mind.	☐	☐
3	I have never sought anyone's counsel unless I have had a really serious problem.	☐	☐

4 I tend to make up my mind quickly with only a little information. ☐ ☐

5 People frequently confide their problems and difficulties with me. ☐ ☐

6 I'd rather be told the truth even if it showed I was not right. ☐ ☐

7 When arriving at a decision I seek the views of my partner, colleagues, friends etc. ☐ ☐

8 People often say that I ask too many questions. ☐ ☐

9 I like routines in my life and tend to stick to them. ☐ ☐

10 Other peoples' opinions are an invaluable aid to my decision making. ☐ ☐

11 I listen unconditionally and put my prejudices and prejudgments to one side. ☐ ☐

12 I always try to see things from the other person's point of view. ☐ ☐

45

If you answered 'yes' for all of these, then go back and do it again because there are too many inconsistencies.

If you answered 'yes' to 1, 2, 5, 6, 7, 8, 10, 11 and 12 then you have your prejudices well under control. However, be careful because your success as a leader depends on how able you are to really think with an open mind – and only you can take steps in that direction. We all tend to think that we are a lot more objective and open minded than we really are.

No one really knows how you think, solve problems, or create opportunities for yourself, people will only see the results or lack of them.

So seek feedback and information from those you work, live and play with and where they think your prejudices really lie.

If you are a manager, your colleagues and subordinates have probably recognized your prejudices long ago. They may not speak up about it, but they will be making allowances for it and their reactions may reduce the effectiveness of their output. So do beware of your prejudices and particularly bear them in mind when looking at the new skills you need to learn in chapter 9.

How good are you at Communicating?

We spend up to 80 per cent of our waking hours using four basic communication skills; writing, reading, speaking and listening. The greater part of this time is listening, something like 50 per cent. Good communication skills are an essential part of inter-personal behaviour and yet many people concentrate more on the reading, writing and speaking part rather than listening.

We listen in bursts. Most of us are unable to listen closely to what is being said for more than sixty seconds at a time. We concentrate for a while, our attention lags, then we concentrate again. Yet have you ever received any specific training in improving your listening skills. We doubt it! Roberta Cava[1] identified a number of blocks that can distract you when you are listening. Are any of these a problem to you?

- you could not understand the speaker's words because they were using buzz words or jargon
- you were busy thinking of what you were going to say next
- you disagreed too strongly with the speaker's views to pay attention to what they were actually saying
- you only heard what you wanted to hear. (Go back and test those assumptions!)
- you were just too tired to pay attention
- you were distracted by outside noises or movements
- the presentation skills of the speaker were poor – too slow, rambling, etc
- you were side tracked by one particular aspect of the speakers talk
- you could not understand their accent or it was hard work-out
- you were swamped by too much information.

[1] *Dealing with Difficult People*, Judy Piatkus Ltd, London, 1990.

Be aware of these blockages and seek to overcome them. If the speaker uses jargon ask them to use simpler language. Listen to what someone has to actually say before deciding on your answer. Before deciding how much work you have to do in this area, test how good a listener you are.

Rate yourself using the following scale:

Factor	Score				
	Always 5	Mostly 4	Some-times 3	Rarely 2	Never 1
1 I let the speaker express all their ideas completely without interrupting them.					
2 At a meeting or during a telephone call, I write down the important parts of the message.					
3 I repeat the essential details of a conversation or summarize this back to the speaker to make sure I have understood.					
4 I try to concentrate when I am listening so as not to be distracted.					
5 I try to look and act interested in other people's conversations.					
6 I understand that I am not communicating well if I am doing all the talking.					
7 I behave as though I am listening (ie I ask questions, summarize and repeat points, etc.).					
8 I look as if I am listening in meetings (ie I make eye contact, nod my head).					

▶

▶

9 When involved in conversation with someone, I take note of non-verbal forms of communication such as body language, tone of voice etc., not just the words the person is using.					
10 I try not to become aggressive or highly excited if my views are different from the person speaking to me.					
Total score					

If you have scored 40 or more you are an excellent listener. With more than 25 you are better than average. Anything below that and you require significant improvement. Change winners have excellent communication and interpersonal skills. They want feedback and they obtain this from all the people they associate with. If you are not a good listener you will miss the key messages.

The other major part of communicating is speaking. There are many courses available to make you a more effective public speaker, but the most crucial balance is that between listening and speaking and this will impact strongly on your interpersonal effectiveness. If you speak all the time and do not listen people will think you are not interested and do not value their view point. If however you do not speak well, it will be difficult for you to engage others and to give them feedback and support.

Again rate yourself against the following scores:

Factor	Score				
	Always 5	Mostly 4	Some-times 3	Rarely 2	Never 1
1 I accept that in a conversation it is my responsibility to help other people to understand me.					

2 I try to use language the listener can understand.					
3 I try to be aware when the person I am speaking to is no longer listening properly.					
4 I make sure my non-verbal signals are the same as my verbal ones.					
5 I speak clearly.					
6 I make sure I am not aggressive to my listeners, by speaking too loudly, leaning over people, prolonged eye contact, etc.					
7 When asking somebody to do something for me, I ask for feedback and a summary of what I have said to make sure I have been understood.					
8 I ensure that my listeners know what I want from them.					
9 If asking for help, or giving instructions, I keep my sentences short, sweet and to the point.					
10 I accept it is my responsibility to make myself easy to listen to (ie I stick to the point, I pace myself well, I invite feedback, etc.).					
Total score					

If you have scored over 40, you are an excellent speaker, over 25 and you are better than average. Below this and you need practice and the acquisition of more skills.

The other major parameters that effect communication are the styles of communication and the situational context. These are pursued in further detail in chapter 9 and will give you definite pointers on what you can do to improve.

What is your preferred leadership style?

Reading the current management literature you could not be blamed for being somewhat confused on what is the best 'style' of leadership. Some will advocate outright empowerment with power to the people. Other suggest helping your employees to grow and developing them by giving input into decision making. Others will say that the only true leadership style is via command and control. The truth is that there is a time and a place to use most leadership styles. Successful leaders know when to direct, when to make decisions with input, when to coach and when to delegate.

To help you identify your preferred leadership style we have drawn below 'The Leader's Window.' This is a structure with four small panes for viewing leadership identified by John D W Beck and Neil M Yeager[1]. The diagram shows the varying levels of direction and support you can give, and it gives you a look at the four windows of leadership.

50

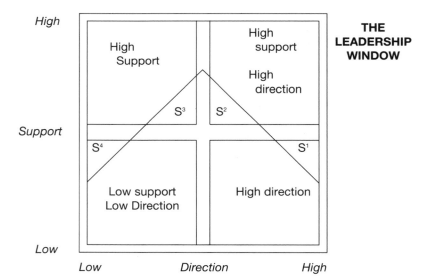

[1] 'The Leader's Window', John Wiley & Sons, New York, (1994).

Look through all four questions and then answer honestly YES to which most closely corresponds to your leadership style. Check it out with your subordinates.

S1 – High Direction

Yes *No*

Do you tell people what, when, why and how to proceed and then monitor and control them closely?

☐ ☐

S2 – High Direction and High Support

Do you seek input from your staff, but then you make the decision and set the course for action?

☐ ☐

S3 – High Support

Are you happy to provide information or opinions, but stress that the person or team you are leading has to make the decisions?

☐ ☐

S4 – Low Direction and Low Support

When you trust someone or they know a lot more than you about a problem, do you get out of the way and let them make their own decisions?

☐ ☐

51

If you answered Yes to S1, this style is most appropriate when workers are inexperienced or new. It is also helpful when people are having trouble getting started on a project, or when they need someone to help structure their work. The danger in this style is crossing over from direction to domination.

If you answered Yes to S2, this is a good problem-solving style. However, there is the difficulty in becoming bogged down in different people's view points and possibly failing to make a decision at all.

If you answered Yes to S3, you are probably good at helping develop people. You ask questions that guide subordinates to make good decisions. You are developing them to assume responsibility. The danger is in perhaps allowing people either to prevaricate or lean too heavily on you for support in very minor decision making.

If you answered Yes to S4, then you are an extremely good delegator. However, at worst you could be abdicating your responsibility.

If you answered YES to all four or more than one style that is good because it demonstrates that you already change your leadership style.

As a manager, you face a variety of situations that require a variety of approaches. In chapter 9 we will show you how to use all your styles appropriately.

How good a team player are you?
■ ■ ■

One of the only sure things about all the changes that are taking place is that working in teams is here to stay. With flatter structures, more participation in the workplace, the changing role of managers and the increasing number of women in the workplace, more team players will survive than ethereal stars.

Effective teamwork means balancing decision-making styles. This assessment will allow you to identify your own style and discover its strengths and weaknesses. We have deliberately not set these questions in the workplace. We are seeking to help you discover your underlying decision making style rather than allowing you to guess the answers that you feel would be most appropriate in the work setting. If you feel that you cannot trust yourself to answer honestly, test your responses with a friend.

Assessing risk

Answer the following questions by selecting your most likely response to the situation described.

1   You buy a lottery scratch card and win £500. Will you:
    a) Buy 500 more scratch cards on the basis that you
       are on a winning streak and could win millions? ☐
    b) Decide your luck cannot hold out and take home
       your £500 winnings? ☐
    c) Buy 50 more scratch cards on the basis that you
       will still have £450 left if you win nothing in that 50? ☐

2   You take an interesting statuette that you bought for
    £5 along to the antiques road show. Whilst there, a
    dealer offers £1000 on the spot although an expert
    says you may get considerably more if it goes to
    auction. Do you:

a) Refuse the offer on the chance that you will make more by selling at auction? ☐

b) Accept because you will have made a good profit anyway? ☐

c) Insist on testing the price with other purchasers not at auction, although this could jeopardize the sale? ☐

3   You contract a painful but non-fatal condition. The doctors tell you that there is no bona fide cure only an experimental drug. This drug has cured similar cases but there have been some fatalities. It must be taken within three weeks of the onset of the condition and you only have a week to decide. Do you:

a) Agree to the treatment immediately so as not to miss what might be your only chance of a cure? ☐

b) Turn it down and continue to search for a safe cure? ☐

c) Risk another two days delay before making your decision to seek another opinion of the risks involved? ☐

53

4   You have fallen in love with a country cottage that is located just where you want it. However there are other people interested so you must sell your own house quickly. You receive an offer but it is considerably less than your asking price. The purchaser will not increase the offer and with the down turn in the market your house could remain unsold. Do you:

a) Turn the offer down hoping that someone else will come along with the asking price? ☐

b) Accept rather than lose this quick sale? ☐

c) Stall for as long as possible to keep the prospective purchaser interested while you seek a better offer? ☐

5   Your daughter has been offered a place at Oxford University to commence in October, but has also been offered a year's secondment to work for the UN in Africa. If she forgoes her place at Oxford this year, they cannot guarantee that the place will be offered in a year's time. Do you:

    a) Tell her to go to Africa, after all there are other
       universities? ☐

    b) Urge her to forget Africa and not to lose the
       opportunity of a place at a prestigious University? ☐

    c) Suggest that she tries to get the UN to arrange for
       a deferment at Oxford? ☐

To score the assessment add up the numbers of 'a's, 'b's and 'c's.

Majority of 'a's

You are always willing to take big risks in the hope of maximum rewards. You approach challenges with optimism and confidence, always assuming you will win.

Strengths – very positive and often see opportunities missed by others. A risk taker, entrepreneurial type. Teams need a positive risk taker.

Weaknesses – high risks can sometimes lead to big losses. You need to be balanced on a team by the far more cautious approach of majority bs.

Majority of 'b's

You always try to minimize the losses in case things go badly.

Strengths – you are excellent at managing other people's finances because you do not take speculative risks, however tempting.

Weaknesses – you may miss the opportunities. A team dominated by others like you will seldom make a mistake, but may achieve little.

Majority of 'c's

Your decisions are strongly influenced by waiting to minimize losses and maximize gains.

Strengths – you always look for the middle course unfazed by lost chances or excessive losses.

Weaknesses – you are always looking for the compromise solutions that can lead to mediocrity of performance.

If you scored near equal totals on all three letters then you have a very flexible decision making style and can adapt to different situations.

To be successful, a leader should combine all three styles in equal amount.

The Belbin team types

The pioneering research on team performance and team types was carried out by Dr Meredith Belbin, at the Administrative Staff College at Henley. Belbin has gone on to produce one of the most widely used questionnaires for team selection and team training and his analysis forms the basis for much work in this field.

The Belbin team types are:

- **Co-ordinator** – mature, confident, balanced
- **Plant** – creative, imaginative, unorthodox
- **Resource investigator** – extrovert, enthusiastic, exploratory
- **Shaper** – dynamic, challenging, outgoing
- **Monitor-evaluator** – serious, strategic, discerning
- **Teamworker** – mild, perceptive, accommodating
- **Implementer** – disciplined, reliable, efficient
- **Completer** – painstaking, careful, conscientious
- **Specialist** – single minded, self starter, dedicated.

Many companies have used this typology and you may well already be aware of your type. If you have not been tested there is a self-completion questionnaire available.

However the important thing to remember is that there is no single type of team person. What is needed is a mix of types. Team members should be selected for their know how, and not for seniority or any criteria related to status. For self-managed teams it is essential that there is a team member who is of the co-ordinator team type to ensure that the team works together to achieve its aims. Chapter 9 looks at ways of developing successful teams in more detail.

Are you a change winner?

■ ■ ■

Honesty time is here. How well have you scored? Have you discovered that you are weighed down with prejudices, a lousy communicator, your preferred leadership is that of a dictator, and your team style is unique! The thing to remember is *not to despair* – change winners are those who have developed the attributes outlined at the beginning of the chapter – they were not born with them. One of the key attributes of the change winner is their flexibility. We will go on to demonstrate that to succeed in change it must be from a realistic assessment not only of yourself, but the current reality of your own organization. The skilled change winner can adapt their style and their skills to 'win' in the environment in which they find themselves. They also know when the time is right to quit.

Chapter 5 will take you through the environment of your current organization, so that when you look at the change initiatives in chapters 6, 7 and 8 you can select the one most appropriate for the reality in your organization. Chapter 9 then reveals the skills you need for mastering those changes. You may find after completing this self-assessment that you are already fully geared up and raring to go. Chapter 9 is merely a refresher course or you may be thinking *help*, I need to acquire all these skills anew. Whichever it is – go for it – because the process of becoming a change winner is now within your grasp!!

The first step is to understand your own organization fully so that you concentrate on your key issues rather than collecting tons of data that is difficult to use.

5

. . .

Tailoring change to your organization

Where is your organization now? · External threats · The type of structure · The organizational life-cycle · A biography of your company · Benchmarking · The workforce · Other major stakeholders · The way forward to change · Success and failure factors for change · Principles of change

You now know the good news and the bad news about yourself. The strengths you have, which are the ladders to climb and those potential slippery snakes of weakness that could cause you to fall from the organizational game board altogether. Before we look at how you can develop your own skills for mastering change we need to help you explore and understand the version of the game that your organization is actually playing. All organizations are different. Throwing a double six in one could lead you to the top of the biggest ladder. On another organizational board the same score could lead you slithering back to the start. Any organizational change must be considered against the understanding of where your organization is now and where it will be in five years time.

60

The major paradox of modern management is that for most of this century, the main purpose of managers was to set up efficient work practices and procedures and to manage the day-to-day operations efficiently and effectively. Continuity, repeatability and stability were what was required.

Times have changed. You, as a manager still have to deliver products and services in the quantity and quality wanted but you are also being asked to orchestrate significant organizational change.

In most organizations, managers are having difficulty learning to balance continuity and discontinuity. The trouble is putting current casualties and crises on hold while you plan and implement the necessary future changes. Where do you find the time even if you, like many of today's managers, are working a twelve-hour day?

Another major challenge is the sheer complexity of the task. Everything is interconnected – structure, relationships, technology, people, values, beliefs, etc. – how can you change one element in the mix without affecting the rest? These difficulties are compounded by the ambiguity, uncertainty and emotion that pervades every aspect of the change process. It is a big obstacle for managers to keep people in a positive frame of mind.

However, before you can decide how best to meet these challenges, you need to understand where your organization is coming from and going to. In chapter 4 you looked at yourself – now you need to examine your organization in the same impartial way.

Where is your organization now?
■ ■ ■

You need to identify for your organization:

- external threats

- the type of structure

- where it is in its life-cycle

- the level of involvement of the workforce

- its overall health.

This will help you decide which change technique or combination of them as described in the proceeding chapters is most suited to your organization.

External Threats

Score your company against the risk factors in the table below:

Assessing external risk

Risk factor	Score				
	Very low 1	Low 2	Medium 3	High 4	V High 5
1 Are your customers becoming increasingly sophisticated in their demands with higher specifications, more personalization, etc?					

61

▶

▶

2 Are your customers demanding an ever-expanding range of products from which to select their choice?					
3 Is the life-cycle of your products and services becoming shorter – ie are your customers always on the outlook for new gimmicks, new cures, new colours and design, etc?					
4 How at risk are you from technological obsolescence? (Beware this is a very difficult one to assess)					
5 Are there many new, more flexible entrants moving into your market?					
6 Are you at risk from world wide competition with more markets becoming global?					
Total score					

High Scores in any of these areas indicate that perhaps you are not as safe as at first you thought.

High Scores in all of them and maybe it is time to take out the life saving equipment.

Low Scores in 1 & 3 suggest you have processes that support speedy development from design to production, flexible production techniques and quality. Therefore you can respond better to threats from those risk factors in questions 5 & 6.

High Scores in 1 & 3 suggest that your processes are out of step with existing needs. If you also have high scores in 5 & 6 you could be dead!

High or Low Scores in 4 are not really predictive because this is the real wild card. Technological obsolescence can hit even the best prepared and can make your products or your processes or both obsolete.

The Type of Structure

Structures can have a big impact on an organization's capacity to cope with change as does their focus. Where organizations are inward looking and focus on themselves without looking over their shoulders at the competition then they are introverted. On the other hand, the horizon scanners are the extroverts. Organizations can combine either of these focuses with being centralized or decentralized.

Let us look at how introverted or extroverted your organization is and how centralized or decentralized

Assessing your type of organizational structure

Tick YES or NO as appropriate.

		Yes	No
1	Do most of the internal memos and letters you receive focus on market opportunities or customer responses?	☐	☐
2	Do you receive a regular press cutting service showing write-ups on your organization and your main competitors?	☐	☐
3	Do you carry out regular surveys of customer satisfaction?	☐	☐
4	Do you know the market share of your major competitors?	☐	☐
5	Do you subscribe to all the trade magazines for your sector?	☐	☐
6	Are the majority of your staff engaged in direct customer contact activities or know the relationship of their activity to the end product and the customer?	☐	☐
7	Do you have more than three tiers of management?	☐	☐
8	Do all jobs in your organization have well-defined roles and tasks?	☐	☐
9	Do you have well-defined operating procedures and processes?	☐	☐

63

10 Do most of the major decisions in your organization get made by the top two tiers of management?

11 Is your main communication system in the organization through management briefing or something similar?

12 Are most of your support functions, eg Personnel, Management Accounts, Payroll, Marketing, a head office or corporate function?

If you have answered:
- mainly *yes* to 1–6 then yours is an extroverted organization
- mainly *no* to 1–6 then yours is an introverted organization
- mainly *yes* to 7–12 then yours is a centralized organization
- mainly *no* to 7–12 then yours is a decentralized organization

So what does this mean?

If you work in an organization that is a *centralized introvert* then it is vulnerable to all the risk factors highlighted in questions 1 to 3 in the previous risk questionnaire. On the other hand, if your organization is a *decentralized introvert* it is likely to be able to respond more quickly to change. However if it is not routinely scanning the horizon it may not anticipate the threats until it is too late. Introversion tendencies can become very strong. The outside world and other ways of doing things are seen as alien and unwelcome. The Civil Service and clearing banks are good examples of introverted centralized organizations.

If your organization is a *centralized extrovert* it will see the threats but find it difficult to respond quickly. On the other hand, the *decentralized extrovert* organization is alert to its customers and competition to see the threats and is flexible enough to turn them into opportunities. Advertising, public relations agencies and consultancies are examples of this type of organization.

The Organizational Life-Cycle
■ ■ ■

Companies, like products are generally subject to a life-cycle. They start small and entrepreneurial with an extrovert focus that keeps them close to their customers. Communications are quick and direct as there are usually few if any levels of management.

As they mature, growth leads to an expansion of staff. Roles often become more specialized and therefore more fragmented, levels of management are added so that there is effective command and control. The voice of the customer gets filtered.

Ageing companies may grow even larger and acquire prestigious offices. More layers of management are added. Organizational politics become very complex and time-consuming. Customers become relegated in these organizations that are often centralized and introverted. If your organization has scored as *introverted* and *centralized* in the previous section and in addition it is showing others signs of ageing or indeed senility then beware. If you fail to diversify or delayer or restructure your organization will become vulnerable to not only its own life-cycle but the life-cycle of its product and its more agile competitors.

65

Pedler, Burgoyne and Boydell[1] produce a useful schematic that shows the life stages of a company (see overleaf).

---

[1] '*The Learning Company*', McGraw Hill, (1991).

```
S                        7 The Transforming company
u
c
c              5 The Wilderness company
e
s
s          4 The Established company


o                                        6 The Dying company
r

              3 The Rational company


C
o
m    2 The Pioneer company
p
l
e  1 The Infant company
x
i
t
y                                              Time or Effort
```

A biography of your company

You can use this to develop a biography of your company. If you look at the key questions listed below for each stage you will get some ideas and suggestions for getting a picture of where you have been and what made you the company you are today; where you are now and what issues you are facing now and where you are going in the future and what your first steps might be.

Stage 1 – The Infant Company – brand new start up by an individual or group or it could be a new venture for an existing company.

Key questions for this stage are:

■ what is the company's vision?

- what is its purpose?
- how can we turn the vision into a reality?
- what is the culture of the company?
- what people, money, equipment, etc. do we need?
- what are our key products and how do we market them?

Stage 2 – The Pioneer Company – small and growing fast with a powerful figure driving it.

Key questions for this stage are:

- shall we stay the same size or expand?
- if we do expand, what additional systems and people will we need?
- will the current leadership style be appropriate?
- will the current leaders be able to cope?

67

Stage 3 – The Rational Company – probably outgrown its original founders, and has become bigger and more complex.

Key questions for this stage are:

- is the management style patriarchal, too personal?
- are the original founders really in touch with what the organization needs now?
- do we need systems for effective command and control?
- do we need specialist functions such as personnel evaluation and research?

Stage 4 – The Established Company – has well established procedures for command and control.

Key questions for this stage are:

- how do we reintroduce risk taking?
- how do we motivate people and remove bureaucracy and red tape?
- how can we encourage cross-functional working?
- how can we get decision making back down to the front-line departments?

Stage 5 – The Wilderness Company – too introverted, has lost touch and lost its way.

Key questions for this stage are:

- can we get closer again to our customers and suppliers?
- should we have a new purpose and if so what should it be?
- do we need to look for new markets/customers?

Stage 6 – The Dying Company – this is where the organization is failing or where it has completed its purpose.

Key questions for this stage are:

- is it time for the company to die or can it be saved?
- can a phoenix be resurrected from the ashes?
- if it is to die what are its obligations to its major shareholders?

Stage 7 – The Transforming Company – this is one that has found new purpose, identity and life.

Key questions for this stage are similar to those for Stage 1.

- what is the organization's vision and purpose?
- who are our new customers?
- what are we going to do differently this time to ensure survival?
- how can we learn from our mistakes?

When you have a feeling of the phases the organization has been through, look for the themes or threads that run through the company's life so far. These are harder to detect than phases. There could for example be themes concerning the type of conflicts experienced, of short termism, authoritarian management style, etc. Themes are extremely important to spot because they tend to survive as undercurrents in the organizational culture and can come back either to support or haunt you in the future.

Once you have identified the underlying themes you need to identify:

- which of these themes survives?
- which are positive ones to build on?

- which are the dangerous negatives ones that need to be watched?

- which positive themes have disappeared and need to be reintroduced?

As a result of this themes work you will have some indicators of how the organization may react in the future.

Benchmarking

You can only carry out benchmarking once you have a true idea of the reality of your organization. Benchmarking compares one organization or a part of it with another. You can compare a process such as design to implementation of a new product or a specific function, eg finance. You can make comparisons within your own sector or outside it. The first step is to understand your own organization fully so that you concentrate on your key issues rather than collecting tons of data that is difficult to use.

The value of benchmarking is that it turns the focus of organizations outwards to fresh ideas and approaches. Even top performing organizations are likely to have areas where they can still do better.

However, there is a danger that managers who do not adequately appreciate their own business processes use benchmarking as an excuse for industrial tourism. They can then make sweeping generalizations about over-staffing. Instead, they should use benchmarking to point out where you ought to investigate in greater depth. Another drawback is that benchmarking can be at odds with re-engineering. It tends to concentrate on relatively modest improvements rather than the dramatic one sought in re-engineering.

You might consider joining or forming a benchmarking club. This will help in making comparisons as you would collect information to common definitions and measures.

The Workforce

The expectations of today's workforce are often quite different to

69

those of yesteryear. They have grown up during the post-war Thatcherite years of the 'everybody for themselves' ethos. With the breakdown of the extended family, the increase in the number of single parent families, the increase in adult illiteracy, the changing racial mix and the increase in the female participation role, those in their twenties and thirties will have learned independence and responsibilities and a particular view of the world at an early age. This will give them different expectations and needs of work:

- they expect to participate in workplace decisions that affect them

- they want information and feedback on what they do and the benefit to them

- they want to be led and motivated, not manipulated and controlled

- they expect companies to provide the skill deficit where schools may have failed them

- they want to be treated as colleagues not subordinates.

But what does this mean for your skills as a manager – how do you motivate this generation?

A lot is talked about empowerment and having an empowered workforce, ie one that is informed and involved. Often top executives ask for greater employee participation without telling managers – those stuck in the middle – how to do it.

How does it feel to be stuck in the middle? It is highly likely that you are one of these managers who is under attack from both sides. How will you go about pleasing bosses who demand even better quality and financial results and also employees who want more say in how things are done, who expect a more personalized and customerized service.

It is possible but you need to understand:

- why you may be feeling at best neutral or at worst negative to employee involvement

- what motivates people

■ what are the options for employee involvement

■ how to create a partnership.

In his book[1] Rick Maurer identifies several more reasons for managers' hostility to giving people more control over their work:

■ **risk aversion** – supposing they do something wrong – everybody will know

■ **punishing offenders** – an executive who punishes people for taking risks or doing things differently can hardly expect them to take chances again

■ **micro management** – they trust no one to make decisions no matter how insignificant

■ **performance appraisal** – particularly if this is geared to individual performance it can be divisive and can ignore the true work environment eg team effectiveness or relationships

■ **us versus them** – The traditional adversarial relationship between management and labour can be so ingrained in some organizations that employees are immediately suspicious of any forms of employee involvement.

Do any of these feelings apply to you? Some must because otherwise why aren't you doing it? Research has shown again and again that empowered workforces produce better results. For example, take Bayanon, part of General Electric. In 1993, they delayered their organization and reorganized their workforce into self-managing teams. Each team owns part of the work with team members coming from all areas of the plant. Workers change jobs every six months rotating through the factory's four main work areas. In just one year of working in this way the workforce became 20 per cent more productive than its nearest company equivalent.[2]

71

[1] '*Caught in the Middle – A leadership Guide for Partnership in the workplace*' Rick Maurer, Productivity Press Cambridge, (1992).
[2] '*The Search of the Organization of Tomorrow*', Thomas A Stewart, Fortune, 19 May 1993.

So what motivates people to produce superior results? Read chapter 6 for more details. Our experience with working with a number of organizations is that any empowerment initiatives must include most of the following:

1 **Feeling of value/self worth** – people want to know that their lives have significance and that there is value in what they do. If they cannot achieve that at work, then they will get it somewhere else. Involved employees are able to feel proud of what they do and have a vested interest in the success of the company because it will mean that they are successful too.

2 **Feedback** – people want to know how they are doing – whether it is good or bad. They also want to see a task through from start to finish so that they can see the results of their labour. The Industrial Society found in its Mori survey in June 1988 that most employees wanted explanation rather than data about matters which they saw directly affecting them. 61 per cent wanted to know how they were performing in their jobs.

3 **Challenge** – people will often rise to a challenge if they feel that they can do something better than it has been done before. Challenge triggers learning which in turn leads to personal growth.

4 **Recognition** – people like to be recognized for doing something well, be it only a pat on the back or winning the employee of the month award. How often do you say 'thank you, well done' to your staff?

5 **Decision making** – people feel motivated when they are able to make decisions about what they will do, how, when and where. You can take a number of routes to greater employee involvement to empower your staff but the most important thing is, that which ever option you choose, it is tailor made for the prevailing culture in your organization.

David Bowen and Edward Lawler Sloan[1] found basically three types of involvement.

1 **Suggestion involvement** – here some people are encouraged to generate day-to-day improvements that they can

[1] *Management Review* – Spring 1992 (from MIT) Reprint 3323.

implement to make their work more efficient or to serve the customer better. McDonald's the fast food chain uses this limited form of involvement.

2 **Job/task involvement** – quality circles are a popular example of this type of involvement where volunteers typically meet once a week to examine quality issues and recommend improvements. In other examples, groups work together to redesign jobs, restructure work, etc. They have a considerable degree of freedom but higher-level decisions, particularly strategic ones remain the responsibility of senior management.

3 **High involvement** – here staff work in self-directed teams and the organization works in a horizontal style. Teams are the most extensive form of employee involvement. Here all information on business performance is shared throughout the organization. Employees develop extensive skills in teamwork, problem solving and business operations.

You need to select the type of involvement most suited to your organization. The table below shows one dimension on which you might score your organization.

Type of Organization	Type of Involvement
Traditional, vertical, hierarchical, highly prescribed working practices and procedures	Suggestion Involvement
Delayering organization: strategic decision making still with managers	Job/Task Involvement
Horizontal Organization: information shared up, down and across.	High Involvement

Before moving towards any form of involvement the first thing you need to do is form a partnership with your staff. The skills needed to do this are outlined in chapter 7, 'Skills for Mastering Change.'

73

K SHOES LTD, CUMBRIA, ENGLAND

In 1985 imports only accounted for 9 per cent of the UK Shoe Market. Then came the Italians, then the Asians. By 1992, imports totalled 70 per cent of the market.

K Shoes, a manufacturer with retail stores knew it had to change to survive. It first tried all the usual approaches – squeezing waste out of the system, by automating many operations, asking employees to work harder and downsizing. For a while it worked, but although highly profitable K Shoes was a high volume producer in a market that was becoming increasingly niche-orientated.

Managers at K Shoes studied the processes at the highly-successful US Shoes where they saw small teams of operators perform five or more functions. They performed work with fewer people and virtually eliminated work-in-progress. This was in stark contrast to K's operations that took 150 separate operations to make, box and transport shoes.

Over time K Shoes cut down its many operations into a few modular procedures that could be handled by self-directed teams of cross-trained members. It hopes eventually to move a pair of shoes through the factory in half a day instead of twelve.

So far results are impressive. At its best plant, on-time delivery has gone from 80 per cent to 97 per cent. Productivity per employee is up 19 per cent. Reject rates of 0.5 per cent are now 250 parts per million.

Source: *Inside Teams* by Richard Wellins, William Byham and George Dixon – Jossey Bass Inc. (1994).

74

Other major stakeholders

In the previous section we have discussed in detail the involvement of one major set of stakeholders – the workforce, but of course there are a number of others. The impact of change cannot be assumed to be the same in all individuals and groups either within the organization or outside it. People will behave differently according to their degree of involvement and their vested interests. It is therefore essential that all other major stakeholders are identified. They could include:

- shareholders

- unions

- suppliers

- customers

- the local community.

Stakeholders will vary in their ability and desire to influence change, dependent on the source of their power. This may come from:

- technical/functional skills

- legal/policy control

- status and/or authority

- external influence/credibility

- control over resources

- informal power base.

75

In case you are wondering why we have not identified shareholders as being the most important stakeholder it is because we believe that organizations can only be successful by treating shareholders as only one of the main constituents vital for their success. It is not that they can be ignored, it is only that their interests' can only be served by putting them on a par with the other stakeholders. This is because an organization can only really succeed through its customer orientation and harnessing the collective knowledge of its workforce. This developed as a key theme in Robert Waterman's book[1].

To understand the way in which stakeholders may choose to use their influence you need to carry out a stakeholder analysis for your own organization. This technique is explained in great detail in chapter 10, 'Influencing the direction of change.' It will highlight those whose commitment is essential for change to happen.

[1] 'The Frontiers of Excellence, Learning From Companies That Put People First', Nicholas Brealey Publishing, London (1994).

However, you must never underestimate the power and influence of stake holders. For example, where the change is a fundamental service, eg health, public transport, water, etc., then customers/consumers would see themselves as prime stakeholders. Where there is the danger of possible pollution, as Shell found to its cost in June 1995, with its plan to submerge an obsolete oil platform in the Atlantic, then stakeholders can constitute not only the local community but international governments as well. Identify your stakeholders and then work at how you are going to get them on board with the proposed change.

The way forward to change
■ ■ ■

Hopefully by now if you have gone through the previous sections honestly you will be aware of:

- ■ how vulnerable your organization is

- ■ the potential risks it faces because of its structure

- ■ where it is in its life-cycle

- ■ how healthy it is

- ■ how involved your workforce really is

- ■ how committed your major stakeholders are.

Depending on how you scored you are probably busy scanning the vacancy columns, phoning round the head-hunters or breathing a sigh of relief. But remember chapter 1 – No organization is safe – your winning strategy is to become a change winner.

No change is no option in today's world.

Do you still want to be a change winner?! Maintaining the status quo may feel the most comfortable in the short term, but in fact it is the highest risk strategy of all. There are many examples of people and organizations who were ahead of the pack, but became complacent and stayed still too long, while others invested extra effort and overtook them. No change is no option in today's world.

So where do you begin in your own organization? Change is a learning process. You have to make the discoveries yourself. You can benefit from the experience of others, but you have to work through the ideas so that they fit your organization.

In chapters 6, 7 and 8, we will outline the latest management fashions, but only you can decide the best combination for your own organization.

However before looking at particular techniques you need to assess the forces for and against change within your own organization. This is so that you can concentrate effort where it will bring the best return. The objective is to highlight and strengthen the factors for change and weaken the negative influences. This approach of force field analysis was developed by Kurt Lewin. To do this describe the current situation in your own organization and the change that is required to bring it to the desired future state. Then identify the relevant forces within the organization, distinguishing between driving forces which can be seen to facilitate and retraining forces which are inhibiting. An example of what these might include is shown below:

Forces for and against change

For	*Against*
Increased pressure from competitors	Long standing traditions
Create security through lower costs	Demarcation between staff group
Can fund more training schemes	Traditional training
Scope to increase pay	Disturbs pay differentials
Job enrichment through multiskilling	Union status threatened
Money released for investment	Potential staff reduction

Careful consideration needs to be given to the tactics adopted. If the driving forces only are strengthened, forcing through change, tension will result, and the restraining forces will increase. If however, the restraining forces within your control are weakened or eliminated, stable, long-term change can be achieved.

Success and failure factors for change

The following questions attempt to ascertain how many success and failure factors associated with change are present in your organization. Please tick response a) or b) which ever more closely corresponds to the situation in your organization – towards future change or the way change has been addressed in the past.

1 Who takes responsibility for leading change?
a) Commitment and leadership comes from the top. ☐
b) It is usually led by project managers drawn from middle management ranks. ☐

2 Who gives the direction to change?
a) There is a clear vision from the top reinforced by the actions of top management.
b) Top managers believe in 'don't do as I do, do as I say!' ☐

3 Are new strategies introduced consistent with existing strategies?
a) New and existing strategies support each other ☐
b) New and existing strategies are in conflict with each other ☐

4 Are project management skills available within the organization? ☐
a) Competencies are available at all levels. ☐
b) There is inadequate provision. ☐

5 What is the timescale for the implementation of change? ☐
a) There is a long-term commitment. ☐
b) Managers are looking for a quick fix. ☐

6 Are adequate time and resources given to change management? ☐
a) Staff time is freed up for change activities. ☐
b) Change is just another objective added on to a long list. ☐

7 How good are communications in your organization?

a) There is a free flow of information in all directions. ☐

b) Information is power and people cling on to it. ☐

8 Is training and development available for all staff. ☐

a) Training is available for all on a regular basis. ☐

b) Training is predominantly available for top people when they want it. ☐

9 What level of staff participation do you have? ☐

a) We solve problems together. ☐

b) We tell staff the solutions and they carry them out. ☐

10 What attitude to change prevails in your organization?

a) Change is seen as an opportunity – people want more of it. ☐

b) A feeling of phew, I have survived that change, now I can get back to normal. ☐

11 Do you evaluate the effectiveness of all changes made in the organization? ☐

a) There is a before and after evaluation of all key factors including customers. ☐

b) It is an act of faith – there is no monitoring. ☐

If you ticked mainly 'a's' then you have more success factors present – mainly 'b's' and change is almost doomed to failure. However this only provides a guide and does not offer an absolute guarantee either way. It merely points to those failure factors which mean that to give change a chance of success you need to do things differently.

You will now have completed the diagnosis of where your organization is:

■ its vulnerability in the market place

- the responsiveness of its structure

- its stage in its life-cycle

- its general health

- the degree of involvement of its staff

- its major stakeholders

- the forces for and against change

- the number of success and failure factors for change that are present.

This is all terribly interesting, but what do you do with it? We intend to give you some general principles with regard to change, and then give you some pointers on which of the latest management fashions or combinations of these will best fit your organization, bearing in mind the above diagnosis.

You will now know the snakes and ladders for your organization. First of all you need to discern from your diagnosis what degree of manager's involvement do you truly have. Is it total involvement as described by Bowen and Lawler in that staff are true architects of change where they jointly develop the vision and then turn this into reality? Or are we really talking about architectural technicians where the vision is bestowed on them but staff are involved in how it is realized? If your degree of involvement is only that of suggestion, then really your staff can only be labourers of change. They will merely implement other people's plans keeping a low profile. They will not feel motivated to point out even obvious flaws that they come across. When you look at the management fashions in the following chapters a major deciding factor will be the level of involvement of staff required by the different approaches. For example, it would be suicidal if your organization undertakes a suggestion involvement to launch into the model of self-managed teams with total empowerment, unless you do this in tandem with a major cultural change programme.

To help decide against the diagnosis you have carried out earlier we have produced a check list of which of the latest management fashions might be indicated for you and your organization. This is a quick guide only and some of the suggestions are open to different views and interpretations. However, it does give you some initial pointers.

Key:
EMP = empowerment
TQM = total quality management
BPR = business process re-engineering

1 Commitment and leadership for change comes from the top.

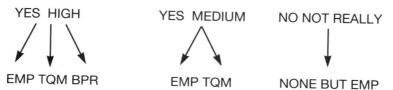

| YES HIGH | YES MEDIUM | NO NOT REALLY |
| EMP TQM BPR | EMP TQM | NONE BUT EMP |

2 What is the direction of change in your organization?

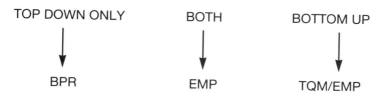

| TOP DOWN ONLY | BOTH | BOTTOM UP |
| BPR | EMP | TQM/EMP |

3 Is the commitment to training and development high?

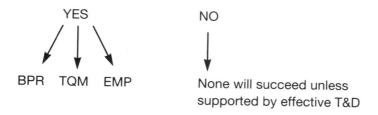

| YES | NO |
| BPR TQM EMP | None will succeed unless supported by effective T&D |

4 What level of staff participation do you have?

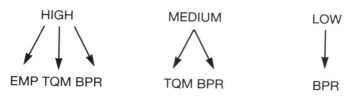

| HIGH | MEDIUM | LOW |
| EMP TQM BPR | TQM BPR | BPR |

5 What resources are available for implementation in your organization?

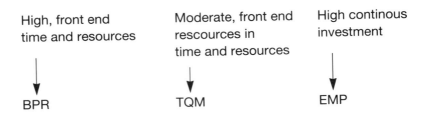

High, front end
time and resources

↓

BPR

Moderate, front end
rescources in
time and resources

↓

TQM

High continous
investment

↓

EMP

6 How rigid is your staffing structure?

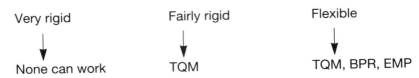

Very rigid

↓

None can work

Fairly rigid

↓

TQM

Flexible

↓

TQM, BPR, EMP

82

These questions begin to give you a flavour of the attributes or the plus factors that are around in your organization to support any of the following changes. If very few are there, the general health of the organization is poor, it is vulnerable in the market and is at a bad stage in its life-cycle then there is no doubt that although change is essential it is going to be painful and difficult. The preparation for change is even more important in this situation so ensure that the principles for change outlined below are embraced before moving on.

These approaches to bringing about change are explored in detail in chapters 6, 7 and 8.

Principles of change

The principles of change are:

■ leadership from top

■ consistent behaviours: walking the talk

■ project planning

■ adequate resources

■ clear sense of priorities

- project teams with staff from all levels

- monitoring outcomes.

A word of caution. You cannot prepare too much for change. In the same way as when decorating your house, the end result is dependent upon time spent on preparation. Those who succumb to short cuts and do not fill the cracks and smooth the woodwork discover that what looks fine for the first few weeks of sun, flaking and peeling will start as the harsher elements are blown their way. The organizational cracks of different interest groups, agendas, etc., cannot be plastered over by a clever PR launch of how things are going to be different. People will only be convinced that real change has taken place when managers do not revert to old behaviour when the difficult climatic conditisations of 'winter' arrive.

You should also watch out for those staff and managers who make a great display of signing up to change but never actually achieve it. They are like the potential house decorator who buys the paint, the brushes and sets out the major steps. However, they never actually start because the weather is never good enough, the paint is not quite the right shade, there are too many cracks and they have run out of polyfiller. These people will still be deciding on the organization colour scheme when the building falls down!

83

People must be shown that not to change is not an option. A compelling vision of the future may not be sufficient to persuade enough people to come on board. Change can be risky. It is often only when the risk associated with standing still appears greater than the risk of change that the waverers will be prepared to make the commitment. It is therefore essential that you involve other colleagues, particularly those who are somewhat risk averse, in your diagnosis of your own organization. This is especially true if your organization is centralized with an introverted focus because many managers may be totally unaware of both the threats and opportunities available. They need the fear of those threats to give them impetus for change.

Where you and your organization will be in five years time depends on how well you apply the lessons learnt in the following chapters.

Empowerment is something that staff need to take and develop for themselves.

6

■ ■ ■

Empowerment

**What is it? · why empowerment? · what does it mean to you
and your organization? · implementing empowerment ·
measuring results · how to avoid failure**

What is it?
■ ■ ■

Empowerment has become the miracle ingredient that fashionable organizations claim to possess. Like many other extravagant claims, the actually achievements are often more modest. Empowerment covers a wide range of practices and is not easy to define. Essentially, it involves sharing power throughout the organization. First-line staff should have the authority to make most every day decisions, without reference further up the organization. Managers are less involved in supervising their staff as there are fewer of them. Their numbers having been culled by introducing flatter structures. Toyota has reduced their tiers of managers from seven to two in many of their plants.

Empowerment involves sharing power throughout the organization

In more radical versions of empowerment, planning is taken out of the directors' suite and becomes a participative exercise. To ensure that staff are sufficiently competent for their enhanced roles a relatively high level of investment in training and development may be required.

Empowerment seeks to enlist the hearts and minds of staff, rather than merely their compliance. The potential is massive as the staff often know not only the organization's faults but also how to put them right. Large sums of money are often paid to management consultants to find out what the staff know already. Good management consultants know this. They spend a great deal of effort talking to staff in humble jobs to learn these secrets.

Another feature of empowerment is the use of teams, some of which are self-managed. Empowered teams are often responsible for recruitment to their teams. They can also elect their own leaders in some organizations and participate in appraising their performance.

Empowerment is something that staff need to take and develop for themselves. This requires plenty of encouragement and patience from the managers. They cannot cut short the process and instruct their staff to be empowered. Some staff may grasp the opportunities immediately, whilst others will take time before they become comfortable with the new expectations. A few may not be able to or be unwilling to make the transition.

The influence of head office is much reduced. Monitoring is based around key outcomes rather than on controlling activity. Head office also supports business units with only those central services that it can provide more cost-effectively and to a higher standard than other potential suppliers.

While empowerment has become popular in recent years, its origins go back much further. Some of the fundamental principles of empowerment can be found in Douglas McGregor's book,[1] He contrasts two opposing views of employee attitudes to work. According to theory X, workers are alienated, unco-operative and dislike work. They have little personal ambition and seek to avoid responsibility. Their bosses have to direct and control them and the employees actually prefer things this way. People also seek to avoid work so that coercion, punishment and direct incentives are required. Theory Y takes the reverse view. It assumes that most employees can learn to take responsibility, to use their imagination and ingenuity, if they are encouraged to do so. However, this great potential is rarely developed by employers. Positive reinforcement rather than punishment is the best way to motivate staff. Staff can become self-directed and self-controlled when they are committed to the organization's goals. This is very much in line with the thinking of the TQM guru, Deming whose contribution we will review in the next chapter.

A key precondition for real empowerment is trust. Managers need to trust their staff so that they can learn from their mistakes without feeling threatened. This prevents the development of a culture of mediocrity where avoiding blame is more important than taking risks to achieve for success. Staff also need to trust their top managers to give them job security. Otherwise they will not come up with ideas to increase efficiency as they will fear that they will be making themselves unemployed.

[1] *The Human Side of Management* published by McGraw-Hill 1960.

In highly-empowered organizations, staff are involved in or completely control a wide range of activities that were previously the preserve of managers.

Which of the following does your organization seek to empower staff to carry out?

Activity	Questions that need to be addressed
Planning and strategy	What should be done?
Process control	How should work be done?
Work allocation	Who should do it?
Work monitoring	Who measures performance?
Control over financial resources	Who authorizes expenditure?
Recruitment and selection	Who should recruit and select co-workers and teamleaders?
Staff rostering	When should staff work?

You can implement empowerment as a strategy in its own right. Alternatively, you can combine it with total quality management as they both depend heavily on co-operation and communication at all levels. Re-engineered organizations can also empower their staff. However, much depends on whether re-engineering results in a high level of redundancies. This would poison the atmosphere and make empowerment much harder to achieve.

Why empowerment?

Empowerment can help your organization become a customer-orientated organization by responding more quickly to their needs. If they query a bill or want to return an unsatisfactory product, they want an immediate response. Having to wait for it to be referred up the line only adds to the customer's sense of dissatisfaction. Empowered organizations can give customers a higher level of service as front-line staff have the responsibility and the authority to resolve such problems. For organizations operating in very dynamic environments, teams can offer much greater flexibility than rigid organizational structures as they can be set up, changed and disbanded with ease.

Empowerment can save money and time by reducing the checking work of supervisors and middle managers. Much of this role adds little value to the organization. The 'savings' they make through their supervision are often less than their salaries, let alone their full employment cost, including pension contributions and national insurance. Therefore, costs are cut by having fewer managers. TQM takes this a step further. This type of supervision is not needed if staff 'get it right first time'. In addition, TQM cuts out wastage, errors and rework as staff know that they are personally responsible for the quality of their own work. Efficiency is increased as staff seek to improve working practices continuously. This proactive approach makes it easier for them to accept change. Turnover and absence are often reduced as staff feel in greater control of their working environment because they make more decisions.

TQM reduces mistakes and increases efficiency

89

If you employ knowledge workers, their potential for empowerment is great. Your staff are unlikely to take kindly to being managed more than what they consider is necessary. If they feel disaffected, they have plenty of expert power at their disposal to take their dissatisfaction out on the organization. For example they can severely disrupt its smooth running through the questioning of management decision-making and possibly using misinterpretation. Less educated workers are also less willing to accept 'micro' management in todays environment where people are brought up to question authority. When workers are not consulted about making decisions, they will not feel responsible for the outcomes. Empowerment will help you to galvanize everyone's contribution to your organization.

EMPOWERMENT AT PROCTER AND GAMBLE, AUGUSTA, USA

Procter and Gamble increased productivity by between 30 to 40 per cent when factories successfully introduced empowered teams. This radical strategy and degree of success are all the more remarkable for an organization founded 150 years ago. It also shows that very large organizations with global sales of about $30 billion are capable of change.

When they discovered that empowerment led to large increases in productivity in the early 1960s, they kept it as a commercial secret as they considered it gave them a big advantage over their competitors.

The organization used to be run on military lines with the 'troops' taking orders from their managers. This grated with a key manager who had just left the armed services and did not want to join another army. The many procedures and rule books were felt to stifle initiative. In spite of the controlling environment disaffected staff could get away with skiving. McGregor was called in to put his theory Y into practice.

To help build more of a team spirit between staff, meeting rooms were added to the plant. Communication was improved by a thirty-minute meeting between the new and the old shift. Working patterns were changed to include and overlap between shifts. All types of news were shared with the staff, including the bad. The objective was to make staff at all levels knowledgeable about the company's fortunes and plans. Self-managed teams of about a dozen staff were set up. Multiskilling and skill-based pay were introduced. Pay progression depended on the views of peers and not superiors. Managers and technicians wear the same uniforms and receive very similar benefits packages. The number of managers was reduced and those who remained changed their role to that of leader. The key improvement was that employees became much more flexible and able to accommodate change.

This model was introduced to the company's worst performing plant where it met with huge resistance from managers and staff. It was only after the employees were told that the plant was unviable and faced closure that things began to change. A survey of their attitudes then showed that they were dissatisfied with the status quo. Five years later that plant too increased its productivity by 30 per cent.

Source: summarized from *The Frontiers of Excellence* by Robert Waterman, published by Nicholas Brealey (1994).

What does it mean to you and your organization?

Empowerment can offer your organization greater flexibility. It is as if you suddenly switched from playing classical music in an orchestra to playing jazz. The customers in the audience set the tone and the players extemporize around it, each making their unique contribution in turn. This can be quite unnerving at first as the familiar forms of leadership are no more. The players are on their own yet play together. Roles and expectations are no longer clear cut. For the conductor and lead violinist the shock is even greater. The future for them is in coaching their musicians and only providing a lead when special circumstances require it. This takes a great deal of commitment from all concerned.

There is a risk that middle managers and supervisors may undermine it as they have most to lose. Trade unions may also be uncooperative as they feel that it is an employer strategy to increase the allegiance of staff to the organization at their expense. Added to this, empowerment is easy to subvert as it requires the full commitment of all staff. This gives opponents negative power.

The form and degree of empowerment can vary significantly between organizations. In the following case study, Honda emphasizes an egalitarian approach. Unlike Procter and Gamble, they had a greenfield site and could recruit staff with their approach to work very much in mind. They could also select young staff who had been less exposed to traditional working practices. However, Procter and Gamble went further than Honda in some areas such as pay progression as they used peer assessment. Both organizations invested heavily in communication.

EGALITARIAN PRACTICES AT HONDA, UK

All staff, including the managing director wear overalls. In emergencies, any member of staff is expected to do whatever task is asked of them, regardless of their status. There are no 'workers' or 'directors' and all staff are called associates. They are all covered by the same pension scheme, sick pay conditions and annual leave entitlement. There are no formal job descriptions. Everyone uses the same canteen and changing rooms. Senior recruits spend at least one month on the shop floor.

Japanese staff trained new recruits who then cascade training throughout the organization. Teams learn themselves how best to organize their work. Therefore there is no role for work study engineers. There are 52 continuous improvement circles each with six members focusing on topics such as new ideas, training and safety.

Staff are briefed at the start of the shift each day and at the weekly management meetings. There are monthly review meetings for all staff with top management and monthly meetings with the chief executive and director for all staff with a birthday in that month. There are regular meetings for all staff for a 'free, frank interchange of views.'

Trust plays an important role. When management reduced the hours of work from 40 to 37 hours a week, they asked their staff to make up the difference through increased efficiency. They responded with plenty of suggested improvements.

Source: summarized from the *Financial Times*, 9 November 1992, p. 10.

Implementing empowerment

■ ■ ■

Changes to organizational structure

Empowered organizations tend to reduce both the layers of managers and the numbers of managers in each tier. This can be very traumatic for all concerned. Much of the success of empowerment depends on whether this is done humanely so that the staff morale does not collapse. The remaining managers will have more direct reports to encourage them to focus on outcomes and find solutions to problems that their staff cannot resolve for themselves.

How teams are run

In really empowered organizations with teamleaders, they are elected by their colleagues. This is the case in some parts of the Rover Group where a leader would support a team of 15 to 20 production associates. Some other organizations rotate this role between team members. Another model is to set up self-directed teams that dispense with the role of a leader. Problems are solved by discussion and the teams themselves decide who should carry out the follow-up action. Rather than feeling that one approach is better than the other, you need to ask yourself, what would work more effectively in your own organization? If rapid decisions are needed, it is probable that teamleaders are required. You do not have the time to discuss decisions in depth and then come to a collective agreement. Team members should typically decide for themselves staff rotas, overtime and annual leave arrangements. This should help to reduce absenteeism as they are less likely to have clashes between their work and private lives.

Decision making

This is the real test of empowerment: what decisions can staff make without upward referral. This would include everyday decisions. This is made possible by reducing the number of rules and procedures as much as possible. Where they are needed, they are agreed by the staff themselves with the aim of improving goods and services for customers. Staff are given budgets so that they can buy what they need to do their jobs more effectively without having to seek prior approval. They can then respond to emergencies immediately. Previously, the delay caused by gaining approval would have been at the expense of the customer or in lost production. Staff should also be directly involved in choosing replacing equipment. They have more idea of their operational needs and they would be more committed to making the most of the new purchase.

Information

Information is the oil that needs to flow throughout the organization to lubricate decisions. When monitoring and project management are devolved to staff, they require regular information to support them. They may need a wider range of information covering outcomes as well as the more usual information about inputs. Staff should be taught how to understand strategic financial information so that they can gauge the health of their organization. They also need financial information that is closely geared to their own operational requirements.

Training and development

There is evidence that training can reduce staff turnover and increase productivity. The most impressive claim comes from Motorola, who spend $100 million on training. It calculates that for every $1 invested it makes a return of $33.

Staff development should concentrate on making the best use of existing staff. Even where high fliers are brought in, they ought to do a spell in the front line to learn how others experience the organization. MBAs start off as sales assistants with the American retailer, Nordstrom.

Inadequate training is often the main reason why teams fail to perform up to expectations. This can be overcome by training not only in job skills but also in problem solving and interpersonal skills. Enterprising organizations run courses on production, scheduling, purchasing and accounting that are open to all staff.

Planning

Many empowered staff are in a good position to identify gaps in your product range and new opportunities as they are in regular contact with customers and suppliers. You can make the most of this knowledge by involving staff and other key stakeholders such as suppliers in planning. This can be by bringing them together in a conference over a couple of days to think through major changes. Another approach is to involve them in project groups that meet regularly for a couple of hours at a time.

Measuring results

Staff surveys are an important way to measure progress and identify particular parts of the organization or aspects of empowerment that need more support. You can ask managers questions about their behaviour and then ask their staff for their views. The differences can be very illuminating. The next case study is a good example to follow.

STAFF SURVEYS: THE CIBA UK EXPERIENCE

Ciba UK survey of their managers' behaviour covered the following factors:

- ensures openness

- promotes co-operation

- delegates authority

- managers performance

- develops people

- provides rewards and recognition

- communicates effectively

- resolves issues

- encourages innovation

A survey of managers and their staff was carried out and their scores were averaged. The subordinates' were slightly harder in assessing their bosses than the bosses themselves. The survey has been repeated annually, so that performance of the organization and specific managers could be monitored over time.

Source: *Personnel Management*, November 1993, p. 30

How to avoid failure

All the key managers need to support empowerment actively, otherwise the initiative will fail. It is easy for managers and supervisors to wish it on their counterparts and backtrack when it comes to them. Staff will pick this up immediately and feel that empowerment is being treated as a token exercise. They will become cynical and uninvolved. You will need to have the support of a powerful director who would be willing to intervene when other managers subvert change.

Staff need plenty of support in accepting their expanded roles and responsibilities. It is important that you spell out to staff what is expected of them with empowerment. Otherwise, they could become confused and anxious. Some may have become institutionalized into expecting others to tell them what to do. They can then have someone to blame when things go wrong. Being empowered means taking responsibility for failures as well as successes. It may be that some are unable and unwilling to make the change. If after a great deal of support and encouragement they are unable to change, it may be in the best interests of all that they find a job with a more traditional employer.

A major investment in training is needed so that staff are competent and confident in their expanded jobs.

Your pay structure needs to be based on rewarding competencies or team performance. If it is based on rewarding individuals, teamworking and co-operation will be undermined as staff are encouraged to maximize their pay, often by competing against each other. Your human resources director should be fully aware of these issues and be leading this aspect of change.

Checklist

The following checklist sets out the areas that empowerment should address.

Changes to increase empowerment

Feature	From	To
Tiers of management	many	few
Number of direct reports	few	many
Teams with leaders	appointed by management	elected by staff
Highly-empowered teams	managed by leader	self-directed
Everyday decisions	many referred up the organization	decided by staff themselves
Rules and procedures	many	few
Staff rostering	decided by management	decided by the staff involved
Routine expenditure	approved by managers	at discretion of staff
Purchasing equipment	decided by senior professionals	decided by the users
Information on activity	geared to inputs	geared to outcomes
Project management	by managers	by staff themselves
Financial information	circulated to key managers	circulated to all staff
Planning	decided by senior managers with little staff input	Major input from all stakeholders including staff

Further reading

'*The Frontiers of Excellence*' by Robert Waterman, published by Nicholas Brearley (1994).

'*Competitive advantage Through People*' by Jeffrey Pfeffer, Harvard Business School Press, (1995).

TQM involves a complete change in attitudes and behaviour throughout the organization.

7

Total quality management

What is it? · how does it affect your organization? ·
how will it affect you? · how to do it

What is it?
■ ■ ■

Total quality management (TQM) is a philosophy for continuously improving products and services for customers. Empowered workers monitor their own performance against clearly defined criteria and suggest improvements. It is very well-established in Japan where it was first introduced after the Second World War. Numerous American and European organizations have implemented it in the 1980s. TQM is also called continuous quality improvement (CQI). This underlines that it is a process without end and omits the word 'management' to avoid the potential misunderstanding that it applies mainly to managers, rather than all employees.

American companies knew they had something to learn from their Japanese competitors when they sold goods in the USA at below the American production cost. The sale of Japanese products shot up when consumers discovered that they were also more reliable. Many senior executives flew to Japan to try to discover the reasons for this challenge to their supremacy. A typical response in the 1980s was to assume that quality circles were the holy grail that we had been seeking. How many were established in your company? Most failed because junior managers felt their jobs were threatened by their own staff coming up with ideas. They responded by ignoring many of the suggestions from below. Senior managers saw little improvement in results to justify the time spent in group discussion, so the circles were slowly abandoned. We did not understand the obvious that just taking approaches out of context and superimposing them in the Western organizational environment would fail. The Japanese strove harder for zero defects and improved quality while reducing their costs even further. Cheap and reliable Japanese products took an even larger share of Western markets, many of our manufacturers were forced to take a second, much harder look at TQM.

So what did they find? Quality is achieved by identifying customer wants, turning them into standards and insuring that they are met. It means fitness for purpose. This can be deceptively difficult to achieve. Black & Decker discovered a large percentage of the drills that were returned as faulty were actually in perfect working order. Customers had selected the wrong drill for their needs in spite of the extensive range available to them. Clearly, they needed to be helped to make a more informed choice through better packaging.

> *For TQM to succeed, it needs to be seen as a long-term investment.*

For TQM to succeed, it needs to be seen as a long-term investment. The returns of TQM will increase slowly over time as quality becomes part of the organizational culture. It should not be undertaken as a quick fix. However, this presents problems to British and American companies that are driven by the need to produce profits in the short term for their shareholders.

Some of the resistance to TQM is the belief that quality is more costly, that it is an optional extra. This is not only suicidal if your competitors offer quality as standard, but it is also wrong headed. It ignores the cost of bad quality. Many hours can be spent in correcting mistakes. Money can be lost in waste materials. Staff can spend more of their time answering complaints. How much management time is spent on checking? All this adds to your costs. Rank Xerox calculated that the cost of their poor quality was between 20 to 40 per cent of turnover before they introduced TQM. It is a great recipe to lose customers and then to have to run expensive advertising campaigns in the hope of attracting replacements. This is why 'getting it right first time' is at the heart of TQM. The emphasis moves from inspection to detection and then prevention through quality systems consisting of documentation, procedures and operations. One of the most powerful arguments for implementing TQM is when organizations calculate how much poor quality costs them.

101

For some, TQM has lost out in popularity to re-engineering as evolutionary change is insufficient to save organizations way behind their competitors. Nevertheless, many of TQM's principles and approaches that focus on the customer can still be of value to any organization. Merely because a process or an organization has been re-engineered does not mean that there is no scope for further improvement.

How does it affect your organization?
■ ■ ■

TQM involves a complete change in attitudes and behaviour throughout the organization. Top priority is placed on exceeding customer expectations. Indeed, TQM is just as valuable to service organizations as it is to manufacturers as they both depend on customers to survive. This includes internal customers within an organization and suppliers. However, fundamental transformations of this type take years to take root. TQM is a continuous commitment: it is the journey not the destination. Some organizations wrongly think that they can do quality this year and then go on to do something else next year. No wonder they fail.

Cultural change is the foundation of TQM. Staff need to put the customer first. They need to take a genuine pride in their job no matter what it is. One of the staff at NASA who said that his job was to help putting a man on the moon was a cleaner! Improving quality should be central to what staff think and do. It has to become absorbed into their beliefs and values. Quality cannot be left to the occasional brain storming sessions or put on hold to cut corners when work falls behind schedule. For staff to have the confidence to suggest improvements requires the support of a more egalitarian culture. This means removing many status distinctions such as privileged parking places and separate canteens.

Excellent communications at all levels of the organization are a key aspect of TQM. This means listening carefully to even the most junior member of staff. Communications outside the organization are also vital.

Performance is improved by standardizing key processes and by regular monitoring. In this way it is possible to quantify the impact of improvements and even drop those that fail to bring the promised benefits.

The main features of TQM:

■ customer centred

■ culture change

- communications

- counting – regular performance measurement.

TQM AT THE ROVER GROUP

Rover was a joint winner of the first UK Quality Award of the British Quality Foundation. Rover was the only car manufacturer to increase its sales in Europe in 1993 and the first half of 1994 by 8 per cent and 23 per cent per cent respectively. Productivity grew and the average revenue per employee increased from £86,400 in 1989 to £120,000 in 1994. The number of people who said they were proud to work for Rover went up from 69 per cent in 1990 to 92 per cent in 1994.

These achievements were based on developing staff and strategic partnerships with suppliers and especially Honda. Senior staff were inspired by a visit to a Honda plant in Ohio, America. They realized that they could adapt Japanese practices to suit their own requirements. Rover saw that the main ingredients were perfecting design and processes and empowering staff to continuously improve them. This resulted in the 'Working with Pride' initiative in 1987 as part of a total quality improvement programme. The whole process, starting with producing a concept right through to design and development, was carried out by a small, flexible core planning team. Suppliers were involved by incorporating their parts in the pilot cars.

Rover followed the PA Consulting Group's four step approach that consisted of:

- establishing quality awareness through a few projects with champions to drive them forward

- quality promotion: all staff seek to promote quality though not in a fully integrated manner

- quality management becomes part of the business process with staff working to common goals

- quality becomes a way of life when it is both planned and self-sustained. This high level of commitment is essential and is expected of every employee.

Stress was placed on genuine two-way communications such as considering other people's opinions, telling the truth and admitting errors. These behaviours were encapsulated in a well-publicized code of practice.

Vehicles are built to order with a flexible production line that can switch from one model to another. The amount of stocks and work in progress is minimized by just-in-time practices. Suppliers and dealers are treated as part of an extended enterprise. The emphasis is on developing long-term, mutually beneficial relationships.

How will it affect you?

You will feel less in control as a more facilatitive style of management is required. Your staff will be making some of the decisions you used to take. You will be spending far less time checking their work as that is now their responsibility. This can all feel threatening to you. There will be less excitement as you will not be running the fastest team of fire-fighters as you will become a fire prevention expert instead.

You will need to realize you still have a vital role. However, it will be a very different one. You will influence your staff as a role model. You will need to show them by your actions that providing quality for your customers is your number one priority. This may be harder than you think. Many managers have failed because they have not 'walked the talk'. See yourself as a coach and delight in the performance of your team. You will get particular satisfaction from those who might not have made it without your help and encouragement.

How to do it

You can also improve your team's performance by influencing managers and leaders of other teams whose work can affect yours. You might find out that other teams have something to teach you. Perhaps you could arrange for a brief demonstration to your own team. When you are a customer outside work, is there anything you can learn from the many organizations with which you come into contact?

On occasions you will act as an internal management consultant. You might be called in by your team or someone else's to help solve a particularly difficult problem. This in itself is a positive sign that your knowledge and skills are valued.

You and your team will be measured by results rather than by who took the final decision. You will need to take pride in the performance of the whole team, rather than your own contribution. Your status will come from heading up the team with the highest percentage of work delivered on time and with the lowest percentage of defects. This information will be produced regularly by your own staff so that they can have a better feel of where they should direct their efforts.

When mistakes happen, it is tempting to dive in and tell your team what they have done wrong and what you, with all your experience would do to put things right. Count to ten and remember you are now a facilitator. Are your staff going through the right process to diagnose and to resolve the problem? If so, let them get on with it. Perhaps you could congratulate them for their success at your next team meeting. TQM is a solution culture. You might ask them whether anything needs to be done differently to reduce the chance of a reoccurrence. It might be a matter of altering a procedure or providing more training. This is difficult to put into practice if you have experienced blame cultures, especially if you bare the scars. These changes will seem easier to accept when you realize that workers in many Japanese plants have the authority to stop the production line when a problem occurs that threatens quality.

105

By giving staff more control over their working lives, they will feel more valued and they in turn will take better care of customers.

MISTAKES AT MICROSOFT

Bill Gates feels that Microsoft's innovative edge depends on his staff generating masses of new ideas. The sure way to discourage them is if employees live in fear of making mistakes. Instead of handing out blame, he cares about how well people work together to find a solution. When a serious bug was discovered in a software product, he agreed to a costly solution of sending free replacements to 20,000 customers. His staff wanted to dwell on the cost implications but he felt that was a waste of time. The main thing was to learn the lessons and to try harder. He sees setbacks as a normal part of business.

Bill Gates owns up to his own mistakes and being at the top, they can be very costly. One such error was not enhancing a Microsoft product to match a better new rival. The product was Lotus 123 and a powerful competitor was born.

Since then Microsoft has enjoyed a decade of success with many employees never really experiencing failure. This, Bill Gates feels has its own downside as success is taken for granted. To counteract this, he recruited a few managers from organizations that failed. They tend to ask much more searching questions about how projects add value to customers and about the use of expensive resources. The lessons of failure are often more profound than those of success.

Summary of new roles:

- coach
- facilitative style
- problem solver
- innovator
- internal consultant
- customer liaison
- supplier liaison

How to implement TQM
■ ■ ■

Understanding quality

The first step is to sharpen your understanding of quality. What better than putting yourself in the position of a customer. Take for instance buying a microcomputer for your home. You would want it to have all the features you need. If you are going to use it continuously for many hours, a good quality screen would be important. On the other hand, if you want to store a vast amount of information, you would want the computer to have large disk capacity. By implication you do not want to pay for features you would not use.

Having all the features you want, is not much use if they are not up to specification. You will be tempted to throw your expensive screen thorough the window if it flickers and hurts your eyes.

A lack of reliability can be fatal. Just imagine how you would feel if you could not apply for the job of your dreams because your computer did not work.

You might refuse to wait two weeks for a product to be delivered when others are immediately available. You might even pay more to have your purchase delivered when you want rather than having to take a whole day off work.

107

Some companies offer a lifetime helpline service, seven days a week. This could make all the difference if you use your computer mainly at the weekends. If you have a problem on Saturday morning, you do not want to wait to Monday before it can be resolved.

Durability may not be important to you if you are going to replace your computer in three to five years time because it will be obsolete. However, durability is essential if you want a notebook computer that can take a few knocks on its frequent travels.

This example shows that customers differ in what quality means to them. This explains the move to customized goods and services highlighted in chapter 1. It also underlines how only a small improvement to one dimension of quality can make the decisive difference to customers. To be really effective, you need to be able to measure your performance against each criterion precisely and regularly. Only then will you know whether quality standards are being met or even exceeded.

Summary of quality attributes

- features – design quality
- performance fulfilment

- reliability
- delivery
- service, and after sale
- durability.

An understanding of quality gives you the foundation to build your TQM strategy. The first step is to define who your customers are and analyze their particular needs. This can be harder in a service function such as personnel or finance where the needs of different customers can be in conflict. Managers may want a greater flexibility in how and when they spend their budgets than the management accountant thinks prudent. Even with such complications going on, to define the needs of internal and external customers is essential.

Visiting customers – to ask them what they want might be even a bigger shock to them than to you. While this means investing time and effort at the beginning, the results can be impressive. You might be able to save a great deal of time if you discover that a feature of your product can be eliminated as it is of no value to that particular customer. Some of their desired improvements might be very easy to achieve. You might wonder why they had not told you them before, usually it is because you have not asked them! You should encourage your customers to phone you straight away if there were any problems with your product. Think how much better this is than if they were to bad mouth you, go elsewhere or both. They could harm you in the eyes of potential customers if they feel very put out by their experience. You will really know that you are winning when customers suggest how you can make improvements. This will lead to better results and give you and your team extra kudos.

TQM requires that the processes are clearly defined so that it is possible to measure the impact of suggested improvements. Problem solving is made easier by following a process of:

- **plan** – analyze the situation and develop a solution
- **do** – implement
- **check** – evaluate
- **act** – put into practice the learning.

Calculate the cost of poor quality

Calculate the cost of poor quality to your organization. The list includes the material and staff costs of:

- ■ **waste**
- ■ **checking**
- ■ **rework.**

This will help to focus the minds of top management wonderfully and will make the investment in training seem cheap by comparison.

Develop strategy and objectives

These may have been outlined by your top management. However, it is crucial that they are turned into clear statements about the type of organization you want to be and what behaviours are needed to achieve this.

109

Win staff over to TQM

TQM is easier to sell to staff than more radical approaches to change. It is less threatening with its emphasis on incremental change. You can point to many features that should improve the working life of employees. They will have more autonomy and a greater sense of control through empowerment. Many long-standing problems will be tackled. Customer complaints will be reduced and less time will be spent ironing out defects. They will receive more training that will enhance their confidence and competence as individuals and as team members.

Communications

Frequent two-way communications are essential. The more media you can use the better. The most important being your own ears! See chapter 11 on skills for winning at change.

Staff surveys

Periodic staff surveys are an excellent way to assess your

progress in winning staff around to quality. They can cover pride in the job and in the organization, measuring the extent of empowerment, problem solving and decision making, the effectiveness of teams and the quality of training and development. It is important to concentrate on measuring behaviours that you can observe rather than attitudes that are concealed inside people's heads. Analyzing the results by grade of staff, location and department might pinpoint specific problems. Involving staff in the design of the survey would increase their commitment to it and achieve a higher response rate. Anonymity for respondents is essential. Using external agents such as an academic institution or management consultants to facilitate the process should be considered where a greater sense of objectivity is required.

Training

Many organizations prepare for TQM by investing in training in understanding quality, teambuilding, communication skills, problem solving, conflict handling and using simple statistical tools to monitor performance. Rank Xerox invests six days training per employee to explore customer needs and how they could be met. Training staff to do their own jobs is often overlooked. For instance, are your staff adequately trained to carry out their jobs? How many problems are caused by a lack of training? How good is your induction training or is it cancelled if staff are too busy? How good are your own skills. Again check this out in chapter 1.

Develop your quality measures

There is a real temptation to start measuring quality within your organization. Instead, identify the critical success factors for your product or service from your customers' perspective. What makes it special to them and what problems are really trying for them? Develop these into quality measures. For instance, Federal Express, an American delivery company, uses a weighted customer service index to focus attention where action should be taken. A serious error, such as the loss of a

package counts as ten points whereas a minor customer irrita-
tion of a missing proof-of-delivery slip scores one point.

For some organizations a number of customer complaints are
due to defects caused by poor packaging or rough treatment of
goods in transit. This might be very easy to resolve by using
more robust packaging or by a telephone call to your transport
manager. Follow back your product through its main steps
including out to your suppliers. Car manufacturers found that
they were taking the blame for many faults that originated with
their suppliers. If you are providing a service, you will lose customers if they have difficulty in understanding your advice, even
though it might be absolutely correct. It is amazing how many
firms in the financial sector have yet to understand this.

Performance can be regularly graphed against the boundaries of
excellent and acceptable performance called upper and lower
control limits as shown below.

111

Control Chart

Histograms are another performance measure. The following
example below shows the distribution of customer deliveries by
days. It will encourage you to ask how the better than average
performances were achieved and also to question what went
wrong in the cases where delivery took twice as long as average.

Histogram

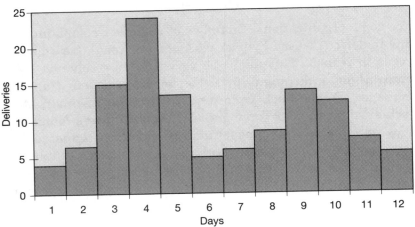

Cause and effect or fishbone diagrams are a very graphic way to analyze problems. They usually analyze causes in terms of processes and procedures, equipment, materials, people and information. As you will see below the effect is on the right side of the fishbone and the cause on the left. Thus, the diagram shows that frequent breakdowns are caused by lack of planned maintenance and life-expired equipment.

Cause and effect diagram

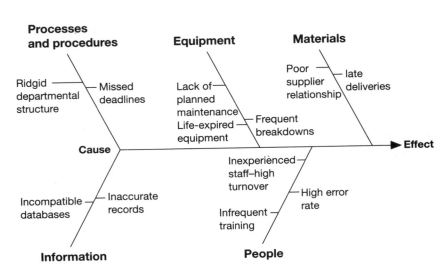

Cause and effect diagrams can then be used to trigger improvements by drawing on a white board. Each member of the team can be given cards to write improvements with one idea per card. They can then be stuck on the board against the specific problem.

Continuous improvement

The first step is to complete the following cycle:

- select output
- identify customers
- establish customer requirements
- translate requirements into specification
- design or improve a process to meet specification
- select monitoring measures
- measure performance
- improve performance through the plan, do and check cycle.

To improve continuously there are various approaches you can follow. You can define what you want to achieve, evaluate and set objectives, plan their implementation, do, check and act where objectives have not been met. This is constantly repeated in order to achieve the next incremental improvement. Procedures are updated to reflect the results of the exercise. Clarifying what you want to achieve may result in changing priorities or targets to reflect changes in customer wants or meeting the challenge of a competitor. The evaluation stage may be lengthy if the causes rather than the symptoms are to be addressed. This process can be helped by asking 'why' to any problem five times. This is reflected in Philip Crosby's, one of the gurus of TQM, approach of defining the problem, fixing it, investigate the root cause; correct the root cause and finally evaluate the corrective action. This is known as the DFICE methodology.

Improving the quality from suppliers

There are large benefits to you in improving the quality standards of your suppliers. If you are not delighted with their quality standards it is unlikely that your customers will greet the end product will much enthusiasm. Your suppliers can add to your costs by delays in shipments and from having to wait for defective stock to be replaced. The best results can be gained by an open, honest dialogue with your suppliers to win their trust and co-operation. This is more effective than immediate threats to move your business elsewhere. After all, why should they make a major investment in changing their ways of working and specifications to meet your needs, if they fear you might go elsewhere at any time?

Becoming a very demanding customer can be very useful when it comes to seeing things from your own customers' point of view. You will know what it feels like to be on the receiving end of a supplier who does not place enough emphasis on customers.

114

Heading up a supplier improvement programme could be a very good career move for you. The growth in alliances will mean that you will be developing useful skills for your future career.

Pitfalls to avoid

There is a danger that in the initial enthusiasm energy is dissipated in an unfocused way over too many marginal improvements. Your TQM initiative can then run out of steam. Your bosses will notice all the busy teams coming up with ideas and will start asking about the improvements to outcomes such as sales and profits. It is much better to focus on those improvements that give customers the greatest benefit or make significant cost savings. It will also give the staff a greater sense of satisfaction to have completed a few projects rather than being bogged down in many.

Some organizations fail to get the full benefit of TQM as they implement it within departments or teams rather than across whole functions. This can be overcome by setting up cross-functional teams specifically for the purpose. Being project manager of such a group may do wonders for your career, so if such a group does not exist, you could suggest to your boss that one should be set up.

Processes can be inadequately documented so that there is a lack of consistency and efficiency in how work is carried out.

Where staff are treated insensitively when their performance falls below expectations there is a danger that they will start 'cooking' the data to fool the management. Alternatively, they will reject ambitious goals as they will be afraid of under achieving.

An excessively bureaucratic approach to TQM can kill off enthusiasm. This has been one of the big criticisms of the BS EN ISO 9000 (BS5750) accreditation scheme.

Summary of pitfalls to avoid

- lack of customer focus
- lack of priorities
- excessive bureaucracy.

115

Learning from others

Benchmarking is a subject in itself and is tackled in chapter 4. You might consider joining the British Quality Foundation, which offers conferences, seminars and workshops, interest groups and publications. You could consider entering the Quality Award! The self-assessment process is an education in itself.

The British Quality Foundation
Vigilant House
120 Wilton Road
London SW1V 1JZ

Telephone: 0171 931 0607

Steps to implementing TQM

Cost poor quality	Calculate the cost of poor quality – even a rough guide will be very useful.
Strategy and objectives	What new behaviours are you looking for? How would you recognize them?
The implementation team	Set up a cross-functional implementation team.
Win staff over to TQM	What do you need to do to become a better role model? What should you do to take a more positive attitude to mistakes? What are the arguments that will win your staff over to TQM? Take them to a successful TQM site. Involve staff in clarifying the new behaviours.
Communications	What are you doing to increase the extent of listening to your own staff? Are you more open with them?
Carry out a staff survey	What subjects should be covered? This can be designed with the help of staff.
Train	What skills do your staff need? When should each training module take place?
Develop quality measures	Who are your customers? Visit them to find out what they want. How can this be turned into standards?
Start the quality cycle	Work back from your customers to analyze and resolve problems, only then improve your internal processes. What are the root causes of problems? How can you solve them?
Improve quality from suppliers	What needs to be done for them to become an extension of your organization? How can you gain their trust? How can they alter their practices to meet your needs more closely?
Learn from others	Find a network to join to benefit from the experience of others. Benchmark your key processes and compare with other organizations.

Re- engineering focuses on improving the main processes of an organization such as design-to-production, production, prospect-to-sale and sale-to-delivery.

8

. . .

Re-engineering

What is it? · how does it affect your organization?
· how will it affect you? · how to do it

The past turned upside down: what makes re-engineering radical
■ ■ ■

We have all grown to accept that new ideas and approaches will affect the way we work. This may cause us some discomfort at first but this usually wears off as we become used to the new rules of the game. However, re-engineering is different. It overturns some of the fundamental principles that we have followed for generations, in fact since Adam Smith in the Eighteenth Century. Re-engineering rejects one of the key ideas behind mass production that has led to the growth of vast industries and our consumer society. It is against splitting up work into small tasks that was advanced by Ford that allowed new staff to become proficient very quickly. Instead, it integrates tasks within a particular process. It has led to large financial savings and huge job losses, in some instances. At the same time, however, we hear that many re-engineering projects, like many TQM ones fail. To predict its applicability to your organization and to decrease your anxiety levels, it is crucial to understand re-engineering and its implementation.

Re-engineering first hit the headlines in 1990 with an article entitled 'Re-engineer Work – Don't Automate, Obliterate' in the Harvard Business Review. Its author Michael Hammer joined with James Champy to write 'Re-engineering the Corporation' in 1993. They state that re-engineering is 'the fundamental rethinking and radical redesign of business processes to achieve dramatic improvements in critical, contemporary measure of performance, such as cost, quality, service and speed.'[1] This might involve reducing the time to produce a product or service from several weeks to a matter of hours. Jobs would be expanded through multiskilling. Less time would be lost as there would be fewer occasions for work to be 'handed off' from one worker to another. For some processes all the tasks would be done by one worker. If this is not possible because a large number of special-

[1] (1993, p 32).

ist skills are required, the process would be tackled by a multi-functional team, replacing functionally based staff and structures. Fewer staff may be required as a result.

Re-engineering focuses on improving the main processes of an organization such as design-to-production, production, prospect-to-sale and sale-to-delivery. Organizations usually have between 10 and 20 processes. Where all processes are re-engineered this is called (total) business re-engineering. However, some organizations concentrate on re-engineering a few key processes, to save organizational effort and upheaval and to contain design and implementation costs. This is called process re-engineering.

Re-engineering involves mapping out each process step by step, showing how long each takes and the number of staff involved. The process is redesigned by starting with a blank sheet of paper and asking the question, 'if we were to start again on greenfield site, how would we do it?' Very ambitious targets are set to avoid the temptation of making minor improvements. After all if, frequent incremental change is the goal, this can be more easily achieved using TQM as we have seen in chapter 7.

121

In traditional, hierarchical organizations staff are split between separate specialist departments, each with their own objectives and priorities. This can lead to misunderstanding, conflict, delay and large amounts of time spent in meetings. Re-engineering restructures an organization by moving staff out of specialist departments into multidisciplinary teams. Staff can undertake more of a process themselves as they undertake a wider range of tasks through multiskilling.

Staff take on even wider roles where they are supported by expert computer systems. This gives the immediate access to knowledge that might otherwise take years to acquire or be even beyond the grasp of most individuals.

BARR AND STROUD

This is an engineering company that has supplied the Royal Navy with all its periscopes since 1916. Its healthy profits turned into losses with the end of the cold war. This forced the organization to abandon its incremental approach to change as its survival was at risk.

A strengths and weakness analysis showed that it was a world leader in submarine periscopes and its thermal imaging to help tanks 'see' in the dark was world class. On the other hand, only 10 per cent of deliveries were made on time. It was overmanned and had nine levels of management. It was highly status conscious with seven canteens and four carparks for the different grades of staff.

Re-engineering was introduced along with computer-integrated manufacture. The 200 job titles were reduced to 30, grouped into four wide-banded grades. Management layers were cut from nine to four and workers were upskilled. Multidisciplinary teams were introduced and functional jobs were reduced. Teamleaders were trained in teamworking, manufacturing management and labour relations. Pay was related to skill which gave very good rewards to important specialists who are paid more than many managers. Layers of management were stripped out when a material resource planning software programme was introduced. Work was monitored on a daily basis. The TQM approach of 'getting it right first time' was introduced along with focusing on quality to achieve productivity savings.

Between 1990 and 1993 the workforce was reduced from 2,500 to 740, mainly by natural wastage and early retirements. However, there were 50 compulsory redundancies.

Some of the benefits include:

- money tied up in stock and 'work in progress' dropped from £22.5 to £6.8 million

- delivery on schedule improved from 10 per cent to 97 per cent

- design changes have fallen from 3,500 to 2,500

- work in progress backlog reduced from 9,000 to 900.

Source: Carol Kennedy, *Re-engineering: The Human Costs and Benefits, Long Range Planning*, Elsevier Science (1994), Vol 27, No 5, pp.64–72.

Re-engineering responds to many of the challenges set out in chapter 1. It maximizes product life by bringing new products to the market quicker through reducing design and production time. It improves the quality of services to customers by reducing waiting time. Re-engineering can meet the challenge of global competition by reducing costs.

Some of you might be asking if it is possible to produce such large improvements, why was not re-engineering carried out before to any real extent? In some cases the computing power and sophisticated software was not previously available or affordable. In earlier decades the global competitive pressures were less strong. However, a telling reason why re-engineering has not been done on a large scale before is because some of its features are so counter cultural to the traditional hierarchical organization. Those managers with responsibility for implementing it would be those with the most to lose through empowerment, flatter structures, non-specialization etc. It is only now that the need for radical change is greater than the threat of losing old symbols of status and power – organizations have been forced to accept that if they are to survive then they must change the way things are done.

123

When re-engineering was carried out in earlier decades, it was due to very specific conditions. Volvo aimed to reduce absenteeism from financially crippling levels to 10 per cent in its plants in Kalmar and Uddevalla, Sweden, in the 1970s. The short cycle, repetitive work of the production line was replaced by teams completing the final assembly of the car themselves. The approach failed as absenteeism remained too high and it took too long to build a car. This underlines the importance of re-engineering producing much shorter product cycle times and this is used as a key indicator for such projects.

The main features of re-engineering are

- radically improved processes
- equipment regrouped to speed up processes
- multiskilled staff
- case workers to undertake a whole process
- computers used to extend staff roles
- multidisciplinary teams

- higher investment in training

- fewer job types

- fewer specialist staff

- flatter structures

- lateral career movement

- wider spans of control

- wider access to information.

LEICESTER ROYAL INFIRMARY

Typically patients with a complicated, hard diagnose, health problem are referred to their hospital outpatient clinic by their GP. This can be an anxious period as patients often fear the worst about their condition and it could take up to 12 weeks before they could obtain a diagnosis. Separate appointments were made for tests with each specialist department and this can take three to four visits.

Leicester Royal Infirmary now offers neurology outpatients all the necessary test and diagnosis in just one visit. This is achieved by providing a range of diagnostic facilities in a patient testing centre that were previously located in scattered departments. The typical outpatient visit involved 122 separate activities of which half did not add value to the patient. They were designed out of the process as they led to duplication, error and delay. The improvements were dramatic and the time between requesting a test and receiving a result was cut from 79 hours to 34 minutes. This was achieved by reorganizing existing technology and did not require a new sophisticated computer system.

The improvements were planned by multidisciplinary teams of staff from all levels within the organization. The impact of re-engineering was reviewed by some of the hospital's customers: 25 former patients who had complained about the hospital, GPs and an academic panel. The support of staff was gained by good communication. It is likely that the main benefits will be to improve the quality of services to patients. There are some cost savings and reductions in administration. It will take several years before the re-engineering work in the hospital has been fully implemented.

What could re-engineering mean for your organization?

Do not be misled, re-engineering is very much a high-risk strategy as most projects fail to meet all their objectives. However, doing nothing can be the riskiest strategy of all. Continuous incremental change, may not be the best option if your organization has fallen too far behind the leaders or where a powerful competitor is about to complete a re-engineering programme. It is not surprising if your organization is considering the tempting gamble of re-engineering.

In fact organizations in different positions in the race for survival re-engineer. The leaders of the pack want to extend their lead. They are helped by a good financial position that makes it easier to take staff on board. There is more scope to redeploy redundant staff in growing areas of the organization. Another likely feature is that they are leaders because they are dynamic and can handle change well. They may have a very successful, well-established TQM programme. This means that there is a good organizational memory about change. On the down side, it is likely to be difficult to convince staff of the need to change. One of the key drivers for change, discontent with the present, would be missing and will need to be skilfully generated. Staff are likely to be sceptical as they will wonder, why change a winning formula?

The pack might want to re-engineer as they could feel that their long-term survival chances are not good. Staff could be convinced by the argument if it were well put. However, they might be suffering from change initiative fatigue and may not feel motivated to take on the latest chief executive inspiration. There might be cynicism about whether enough resources will be put into change to make it succeed. Such organizations would be sufficiently healthy to have some scope to absorb the casualties of change.

If you are at the tail end, your organization has little to lose by re-engineering as it may drop out of the race soon anyway. Staff would need no convincing that drastic change was essential. However, there may be a catalogue of past blunders from other change initiatives. These are likely to be beautifully illustrated by the resident cartoonists and anonymously posted on the notice boards. The more literary minded might take to circulating spoof mission statements. On top of this, if re-engineering were successful, it would quite likely lead to job losses. Alternatively, the organization may have avoided change and clung on grimly to past ways. It takes a very clever strategy to address this in such a way that the staff would come up with some of the ideas that would lose them their jobs. They would see it as turkeys voting early for Christmas!

Type of organization	Likely exposure to change	Experience of change	Resources to absorb redundant staff	Fear of Failure
Leader of the pack	High	Positive	Large	Low
The pack	Moderate	Mixed	Moderate	Moderate
The tail	Low	Poor	Small	High

What could re-engineering mean to you?

There would be management job losses. Some of the surviving jobs would change from functional to general management. Often managers would be put in charge of a process operated by cross-functional teams. A few jobs are likely to be unchanged as most organizations require at least some functional specialists to set standards and bring in fresh expertise.

So what would be the best strategy for you? To hope that the initiative fails and your job and future career ladder survive the chain saw of flatter hierarchies? Alternatively, concentrate on guessing which jobs are likely to be least affected by re-engineering and to work out how you could get one? These are defensive strategies that might even succeed for a while. However, this is rather like those managers who have avoided mastering micro computers. The longer they have put off the evil day, the more embarrassed they are about making good the learning deficit.

A more opportunistic strategy is to volunteer to take a leading role in planning and implementing re-engineering. Ideally this would be as a team project manager, but even seek out the opportunity to be just an ordinary team member. To some of you this might sound as if the turkeys have not only voted early for Christmas, but have built their own abattoir! However, there are plenty of sound reasons to be one of the key players affecting change. You will be very visible to top management and might even be their salvation if you deliver successful change against the odds. You will get to learn a great deal about re-engineering, the theory and the practice. You will also have a chance to improve your change management skills. Your CV will be greatly enhanced if you were actively involved in re-engineering. You will have a wider range of jobs from which to choose, including outside your industry. These are invaluable because even if re-engineering were discredited as a fad in a few years' time, as successful change agents you would be much sought after and head-hunted. You can be sure that re-engineering will be replaced by another big idea. This is bound to happen as right now many 'wannabe gurus' are working on them and publishers have their eyes on filling international airport bookshelves.

How to gain the attention of top management

Come up with a few ideas for cutting out needless steps in a process, but make sure they do not threaten the key players pushing for re-engineering. This is because some top managers are great advocates of radical change for others, but when it comes to their empires they can sometimes hold back. In these cases, the initiative is likely to fail, but at least your stock would still be high. Also use the material from this chapter, particularly the case studies. Their great attraction is that they appeal to the practically minded top manager who would learn some do's and don'ts from them. Another advantage is that you avoid becoming caught up in esoteric arguments about the sayings of the newest guru. Bear in mind that some top managers hear the latest offerings at international conferences, something you are unlikely to match.

How to re-engineer: learning from the experience of others

■ ■ ■

The following steps to re-engineering are based on the hard won experience from many organizations. You should adapt them to meet the needs of your organization and not assume that there is only one way to re-engineer. Learning also means making your own mistakes. If many of the following are likely to be news to your top management, you ought to think carefully how you communicate the ideas. You should appear as an invaluable support, rather than a know it all who would show them up. One such way would to pick one new approach at a time and select them in order of likely acceptance.

Make the case for change

The case for change has to be compelling for re-engineering to succeed. You need to decide whether you need to strengthen the arguments advanced for re-engineering. All change, even change for the better can be painful. You need to make the dissatisfaction with the present and the gains from change outweigh the pain of change.

> *The case for change has to be compelling for re-engineering to succeed.*

Set ambitious targets

Note the dramatic time saving from the Leicester Royal case study of 79 hours to 34 minutes. This is even more impressive when they are both expressed in minutes, a reduction from 4,740 to 34 as the new time is less than 1 per cent of the former. What would be the equivalent for you?

Communicate widely

If after you have successfully re-engineered, you find that your communication strategy cannot be faulted, tell the entire world, as this will be an all time first. Organization after organization wish they had put more effort into communication. Firstly define all your audiences and the level and type of communication that they want to receive. Avoid cutting corners by producing general purpose material that offends few and influences even less. Use every medium at your disposal such as presentations and meetings, in-house papers, notice boards and put out a weekly progress bulletin on your e-mail. If you are not electronically wired up, then it is a matter of producing a circular.

Listen actively to all staff

Strictly speaking, listening is an essential part of effective communication. As this is often ignored, it is safer to tackle it as a subject in itself. It is tempting to assume that the casual nod not only means understanding but full commitment; the staff may have completely misunderstood. One organization made this mistake and after a large amount of detailed preparation some key players vetoed implementation. They said that if they had really understood what the change was about they would have expressed their opposition from the very start. However, if their opposition was recognized from the outset, their concerns could have been addressed so that they would have probably come on board. The lesson is that it is necessary to test out understanding at an early stage. Consider having a box where staff can post their written questions anonymously. Guarantee to answer them in 24 hours and pin the question and answer together on a prominently placed notice board.

129

Appoint a process owner

Many processes are so inefficient before re-engineering because the ownership of the process is fragmented, sometimes to such an extent that it is not even seen as a process. One owner needs to be appointed for each process. Would this job appeal to you?

Involve staff from all levels from each function

To understand a whole process and to move from a functional to multifunctional structure, what better way to start than with a project team drawn from all the functions involved in a process?

It can be tempting to ignore staff at the bottom of the organization as they are sometimes thought to be not particularly bright or motivated. How wrong this can be. They often come up with the best ideas and then have the gall to say they have being saying this for years but no one had listened to them! Project teams can be a great way to discover what you should have known long ago.

Make sure that if project team members are part-time that they do not drop re-engineering as soon as there is a problem back on the ranch.

Improve jobs for staff

A feature of life lower down the line, is that some bloodyminded attitudes are due to the frustration of narrow, boring and repetitive jobs and the feeling that their ideas and views are irrelevant to managers. They often feel that the way to get a hearing is to be bolshy. However, many re-engineering schemes have ignored staff needs when jobs are redesigned. It is important that the new jobs are neither too stressful nor boring. This might result in higher staff turnover with the associated greater recruitment and training costs. Even if staff remain in their new jobs, customers will fail to obtain the full benefits of more efficient processes if staff morale is low.

Re-engineering is a great opportunity to give staff more fulfilling jobs with better development opportunities. This will lead to them to not only supporting change but they may well start treating customers better if they feel they (as staff) are also valued.

Find champions

Recruiting influential champions for change can make your task much easier. If some were former critics, so much the better. Where some staff have the negative power to prevent or delay change, it is vital to recruit at least one champion from their ranks.

Involve customers

As putting customers first is the slogan of our business age, it is surprising that they are not automatically encouraged to play a part in re-engineering. Leicester Royal Infirmary was brave enough to select patients who had complained about the hospital. Although Levi Strauss is highly successful, it asked the shops that sold their jeans what they thought of them. The good news was that the product was first class as was their marketing. However, retailers complained about delivery delays as their shelves were empty too often. Therefore, the manufacturer made re-engineering its supply chain as its top priority. For some processes, the customers would be internal and more accessible. If we fail to place enough emphasis on customers we will not make large gains in effectiveness. As Drucker says, 'efficiency is doing things right; effectiveness is doing the right things and doing the wrong things less expensively is not much help.'[1]

131

Walk and then map processes

You can get a quick understanding of a process just by walking through it and following bits of paper and work in progress. You will be surprised at the pile of similar forms you will collect on the way. This often reveals some bizarre practices that staff have learnt to take for granted as that is how things are done around here. To achieve greater detail, map the process from the beginning and record how long each step takes. Measure the complete start to finish time of the cycle, including the time paperwork sits in intrays and the hold ups when staff wait for others to complete their tasks. Record the staff involved in each step and the number of 'hand offs' to the next down the line. This work should be done thoroughly enough to act as a baseline measure and to understand how your organization works. However, it can result in paralysis by analysis if it is taken too far.

Find a quick win

Achieving a quick win will increase the confidence of everyone involved so that they are in a better position to see through the

[1] *The Practice of Management*, published by Heinemann (1989).

hard times that are to follow. It does not matter if the gains are small, providing they are seen to be of value. Boredom and loss of commitment can set in where projects take too long to come to fruition due to an obsession with detailed planning. Even worse, they can be taken over by the sort of planner who hates messy reality.

Select a process that would make a real difference to customers or costs

After achieving your quick win, select a process where customers would greatly value the hard won radical improvements. They would be delighted by the improved quality, reduced cost or ideally both. There is one reservation, if this process happens to be one with many hostile and powerful vested interests, leave that one to later and select the next one from your list. Avoid selecting a process that might be a long standing problem to the organization, but actually it is not vital to the customer and does not seriously affect your costs. It might be even a product area where the battle against the competition is already lost. In such instances the option of buying it in from someone who is cheaper and better than you should be explored.

Project priority table

Project	Customer benefit	Likelihood of success	Speed of completion	Cost saving	Cost to put in	Rank-ing
A. Multiskill design process	low	high	9 months	£50k	£10k	4
B. Introduce concurrent computing in design	low	quite high	12 months	£1m	£0.5m	5
C. Re-engineer production	moderate	moderate	18 months	£10m	£1m	3
D. Re-engineer prospect to sale	very high	quite good	10 months	£0.5m	£0.25k	2
E. Re-engineer sale to delivery	high	very high	3 months	£1.5m	£1m	1

The above table will help you evaluate each re-engineering project against a range of key criteria. However, it does not remove the need for judgement and ranking is likely to vary according to individual preference. We gave top ranking to project E as it was the most likely to succeed in a short period of time, so this is our quick win. Project D was selected to follow as it offered very high customer benefits. Our third project was C because its high financial return justified the risk. Also the organization would have gained the confidence and the experience to take on greater risks at a later stage. Introducing the new computing system after multiskilling means that expensive rewrites may be avoided as the new working practices could be tested in practice before the programs were written. Incidentally, the information in the table was made up to illustrate particular points and should not be a true indication of the time and cost involved.

Avoid over reach

Sometimes change really catches on and everybody wants to redesign their process. While this might be music to your ears, it will become increasingly difficult to orchestrate the many musicians wanting to play their own tunes. This leads to over reach where ambition outstretches the resources available. Historians would find this very familiar as it is this that has led to the downfall of many empires, so do not add yours to such a distinguished list. Instead, be strategic and carefully prioritize your projects so that they match your resources and management energy.

Develop a supportive culture

Staff should be encouraged to experiment, take risks where they are not mission critical and challenge managers, even you! Brave failures should be treated as heroic acts rather than being met with disapproval, no matter how mild. This will do wonders for confidence and trust.

Have good project management

Some re-engineering projects have failed through poor project management. Objectives need to be 'SMART'—specific, measurable, achievable, results orientated and time bound. This is an area where you should be able to bring expertise. The computer software is simple to learn and to use. However, the skill lies in breaking down the project into a jigsaw of tasks that you understand how and in what order to piece together. This can be done with post-its so that you can experiment with different sequences. Even a simple project management software package will show you whether you need to reallocate tasks if particular members of staff are overburdened. You need to select key milestones to keep everyone focused on the tasks at hand. It is very easy to become wrapped up in the excitement of change and the talkers might begin to win out over the doers. If you are not a capable project manager, it is a competence well worth developing as it will enhance your chances of being selected to lead such projects in the future.

Test new process in a laboratory

134

Once you have designed a new process set up a laboratory environment where it can be tested on a small scale. Important lessons can be learnt quickly at no risk. Once you have overcome the teething problems, show it to the staff who would be carrying out the process in the future. They might be able to find further scope for enhancement. This avoids the embarrassment of making changes in an operational setting only days after it has been introduced.

Training

Training is vital to give the new processes and ways of working a good start. If you are introducing teams, training in teamworking, project management and problem solving is invaluable. Phase the more job specific training carefully so that staff do not have too long to forget what they learn before they put it into practice. The laboratory could be a very effective training resource.

Evaluate

Evaluate the project thoroughly as it will reveal many valuable lessons. The first phase should be right at the start of the project so that all the baseline data can be collected. Sadly, many projects leave this until it is too late and their indicators have been affected by the impact of re-engineering.

Summary of the key steps

Set ambitious targets	Do they radically, reduce cost, increase speed of service or improve quality to customers? How will you know whether they are achieved?
Communicate widely	Who are the key groups? Have you included all media eg meetings, in-house paper, weekly e-mail bulletin?
Listen actively to staff	How can staff get through to you? Do you have small group meetings and a question box?
Involve staff at all levels	Make sure the most lowly are included.
Appoint a process owner	Who would be the best person to unite staff from different functions and make the re-engineered process a success?
Involve customers	Who are the customers for your process? How can they be persuaded to take part? Would it be useful to include suppliers?
Improve jobs for staff	What are their biggest hassle factors and how could they be removed?
Walk through and then map processes	Walk through the key processes and map out in more detail the important ones. Collect base line information for evaluation.
Start with a quick win	Even a very small win is a good beginning.
Selecting projects	Produce your priority table and select a process that will make a real difference to customers or costs
Develop a supportive culture	Encourage staff to take risks within clear bounds
Project management	Set up a project management system with frequent milestones to keep up enthusiasm.
Test new process	Set up a laboratory to test new processes.

▶

▶

Train	Train staff in new processes, using the laboratory where possible.
Evaluate	Were your targets met? What were your successes? What would you do differently next time?

Next steps

■ ■ ■

Once you have exploited the material from this chapter you can keep your eye out for interesting newspaper articles and read books. One visit to a business library with a helpful librarian could provide a lot of material with very little effort from you. If you know of companies that have done exciting things, phone up their public relations department and ask them for any case study. They are usually only too flattered to help you. Even the least resourced PR department could send you press cuttings and this alone would save you plenty of effort.

Some professional associations have very useful networks that you could consider joining. This would give you a chance to learn the inside story from your counterparts in an informal setting. You could also test out some of your own views with them at very little risk to yourself. The Strategic Planning Society re-engineering and radical change group has speakers from around the world on the subject at its monthly evening meeting. Such groups are also a useful source of information about conferences and workshops

Failure and how to avoid it

A growing number of organizations admit that their re-engineering projects have failed. One of the reasons for this is that they do not place enough emphasis on the human factors. People can make the best processes fail or some shaking ones survive. It all depends on how motivated they are to make it work. Organizations that treat their staff as expendable will find that they will not help them come up with creative insights to improve productivity if it means more of them will be made redundant. Therefore, we advise you to add aspects of empowerment and TQM to your corporate change strategy. You should choose these ingredients so that they blend with each other and your organization.

Further reading:

Hammer, M. and Champy J., *Re-engineering The Corporation, A Manifesto for Business Revolution*, Nicholas Brealey Publishing, (1993).

Johansson, H., McHugh P., Pendlebury, A., Wheeler III, W., *Business Process Re-engineering, Breakpoint Strategies for Market Dominance*, John Wiley and Sons, (1993).

Obolensky N, *Practical Business Re-engineering*, Kogan Page, (1994).

Organization

Strategic Planning Society, 17 Portland Place, London W1N 3AF. Telephone 0171 636 7737

137

According to recent statistics, you will probably change your job up to 10.3 times during your lifetime.

9
■ ■ ■

Skills for mastering change

Networking · communication skills · negotiating skills · goal
setting · team building skills · being an effective leader ·
risk taking · coaching skills · encouraging creativity ·
project management skills · self improvement and career
management skills

The times when you could confidently look forward to receiving your gold watch on retirement are over. CEOs and their junior managers alike can no longer consider their jobs as permanent.

According to recent statistics, you will probably change your job up to 10.3 times during your lifetime. No one is immune from economic downturns and it does not matter how secure your feel today, you could be handed your P45 tomorrow. How can you protect yourself? To master change you need to practise:

- looking at problems as opportunities to be creative

- becoming an expert in the skills required in the organization of tomorrow not yesterday

- networking like mad

- setting goals and working towards them

- being a team player and team builder

- using the language and buzz words of your audience.

When you have mastered these change techniques you may still fall victim to the corporate axe but you will be on your way to another possibly better job.

Managers who take the initiative in developing themselves far outstrip those who wait for experiences to land in their laps. They learn faster, develop more confidence in themselves and enjoy themselves more. So do not wait for these skills to be handed to you on a plate go out and get them. Read about them, think how you can use them and then risk trying them out in the workplace. They will help you be more productive, more effective and more visible to those in a position to help your career.

Networking

■ ■ ■

Does it make you shudder at the thought of ringing round all your contacts? Does networking seem like the sport of social climbers? If you answer yes to any of these think about the statistics.

'In a survey of fifteen hundred successful job hunters, 11 per cent said they found their jobs through classified ads, 2 per cent by sending unsolicited resumes and 63 per cent through personal contacts': *Sharkproof*, Harvey Mackay, Harper Business, 1993.

He gives six suggestions for building a network:

1 Work the conventions and trade shows: get yourself known by delivering presentations, asking well-structured questions, talk to everyone you can.

2 Be visible – Whenever you are promoted, take on additional responsibilities or do something new or different such as sending a press release to local newspapers and your industry's trade publications.

3 Make sure you can be found. If you move, send change of address cards. If you marry and change your name let people know.

4 Write articles for industry publications. Editors are always looking for new contributors. If you are not good at writing pay a ghost writer to produce copy from your ideas.

5 Get a job by getting an education. Professors, course facilitators, lecturers all have their own networks and can often make recommendations to other organizations.

6 Keep an index system of everyone you meet, a method of contacting them and at least one basic fact. You then need to explore creative ways of keeping in touch with them.

Communication skills

Why do communication skills have such power? Because everyone you come into contact with – be they bosses, colleagues, friends, family or indeed strangers want you to behave in the way they feel is appropriate. They want you to sound and act according to the pigeon hole in which they have placed you. For example we all have a view on how professionals such as doctors, lawyers, policemen, etc., should communicate with us. If they conform to our view, then we feel content, but if they behave in a radically different way it immediately causes conflict.

People also want us to communicate in they same way as they do in the same style or else they get bored, irritated, etc. But how can you accommodate varied expectations? According to Linda McCallister[1] there are only six styles you need to understand and use: the Noble, Socratic, Reflective, Magistrate, Candidate and Senator. If you can recognize these styles in others and also adapt your own style, then you will be half way there.

How we say something is just as important as what we say. Below we have changed and adapted Linda McCallister's six styles to coincide with those of the six behavioural styles we identify in chapter 3. People behave according to a preferred style – they are likely to use one or a number of the following:

- **Action people:** They use the fewest words to say what needs saying and expect you to do the same. They are speak before thinking communicators. They do not spare the feelings of others. They want their decisions to be swift and unambiguous.

- **Diplomats:** They believe the primary purpose of conversation is to advance the interpersonal relationship. They would rather be silent than say something that would upset the other person. Above all, they want to avoid open conflict. They feel communication should be polite, warm and supportive.

- **Opportunists:** They are ace communicators. Their conversation style is fluent and polished. They need to hear themselves think before they make a decision. Their conversation is a patchwork quilt of anecdotes, footnotes and reminiscences.

[1] *I Wish I'd Said That!* John Wiley & Sons Inc, New York, 1992.

■ **Technocrats:** They like to discuss, argue and analyze every point in detail. They believe in straightforward to the point style of communication.

■ **Strategists:** They view communication as a strategy for survival and success. They make a great conscious effort to control their environment through their communication style. They are supportive communicators who give and invite feedback.

■ **Gurus:** They display a 'take it or leave it' attitude of superiority, leave little room for opposing views, do not admit failure and feel a strong need to expose other people's shortcomings. However, they are often charismatic in their presentation style.

So how does this help you to manage your style? First of all you need to understand which of these styles most closely corresponds to your own. Try scoring yourself against these headings and then perhaps ask friends, family or close colleagues to do the same. You will then know how you look and sound to others and you become aware of the strengths and weaknesses that you may have in any interaction.

143

However, equally important, you will have a framework against which to judge other people's communication style and this will give you pointers as to how you may need to adapt your own style. Remember that everyone prefers you to communicate the way they do and if you do not you are introducing the potential for conflict.

Negotiating skills are a vital part of everyday life.

Do also note that when you are looking at team building (see later section of the chapter) that there are advantages of employing people with a variety of communication styles. Then the team can take advantage of everyone's different strengths.

Negotiating Skills

Negotiating skills are a vital part of everyday life. Whether it is persuading your children to come in and do their homework when they want to stay out and play; when you want to go to the theatre and your partner wants to go out to dinner; when you need to increase your overdraft limit at the bank. All negotiations take skills, but few people have really good negotiating skills.

Negotiation is something everyone engages in to a greater or lesser extent to resolve all manner of differences. Nothing is more central to negotiation than learning how to negotiate rationally and effectively. Various styles, such as how you structure problems, use information, assess situations, and examine alternatives can seriously limit your judgement and effectiveness in any deal.

The good news is that you can learn the skills that will make you an excellent negotiator.

In their book 'Negotiating Rationally'[1], Max Bagerman and Margaret Neale list seven strategies for making good deals. They state that a major stumbling block in negotiating is the lack of information about what motivates the other side. To create the mutually beneficial trade-offs that result in good deals each party must know the other's preferences.

The strategies they put forward to achieve this are as follows:

Strategy 1: Build trust and share information. This is an ideal way of helping parties to examine common interests and build on these.

Strategy 2: Ask lots of questions. Even if they are not all answered you will have increased your knowledge base.

Strategy 3: Give away some information. This is particularly helpful if trust is low.

Strategy 4: Search for a 'post settlement' settlement, ie try to do even better than the settlement you have reached or are seeking to reach.

Strategy 5: Use different time preferences to create beneficial trade-offs. Maybe you can pay off on a deal faster in return for a better price.

[1] Max Bagerman and Margaret Neale, *Negotiating Rationally*, MacMillan, New York, (1992).

Strategy 6: Consider adding issues to the negotiation to increase the potential for making trade-offs. By adding issues to the table, one party may get what it wants in the original negotiation while compensating the other party on some additional unrelated issue.

Strategy 7: Search for novel solutions to the negotiation that do not meet either party's stated position, but do meet their underlying interests. Look for win/win strategies. Further guidance on dealing with conflict and arriving at win/win strategies is covered in chapter 10, 'Influencing the Direction of Change.'

Common mistakes in negotiation

1 The desire to win at all costs. This is quite irrational and often biases your judgement. You will look for evidence that supports your decision and ignore information to the contrary.

2 Commitment to a particular course of action may lead to a competitive, escalatory spiral that makes no sense.

3 The belief that if one person gains the other loses. This is an over-simplification because there are usually multiple issues in a negotiation that each party values differently.

4 Identifying your key priorities beforehand helps you find effective trade-offs by conceding less important issues to gain on more important ones.

5 Holding on to an initial position or belief and not adjusting it as the negotiation moves on. This can prevent the achievement of the optimum agreement.

6 Framing negotiations negatively ie talking about losses not gains. If you put this in a trade union context you refer to how much less the management's offer is to that requested by the union instead of how much more it is than what they are currently earning.

7 The uneasy feeling that you bid too high and your hand was bitten off. For example you make what you think is a ridiculously low offer for a car and the vendor accepts it. You do not feel delighted – you feel distinctly uneasy – have you been taken for a ride?

8 Over confidence, ie the deal is bound to go your way because of delusions of superiority of optimism and of control.

Goal Setting

What is success? Success is achieving goals. Most successful men and women have discovered that this is true and have therefore developed an intense goal orientation. The ability to set goals and draw up action plans for their accomplishment is one of the most important skills for mastering change.

To find out where your goals may lie, make a list of twenty things you would love to do. Pick one or two and work out how you can do them more often. Next, dream about the kind of work you would like to do. Make a list. If your current job is not on it try to work one of your dream jobs into your life, even if it is on a volunteer or part-time basis. It could be the start of a great new career.

Once you have decided what you want to do, set goals and work toward them. Realistic goals will help you handle change because they fuel your commitment.

There are seven major points to remember when setting your goals:

1 Make your goals realistic. Identify goals that are achievable but that require you to stretch yourself.
2 Break down larger goals into smaller goals – remember we can all eat an elephant if we cut it into small bite size pieces.
3 Write down your goals and be specific. Decide what you want to do, how you want to do it and when you want to achieve it.
4 Visualize yourself obtaining the goal. Always think of a positive outcome. What would it look like? How do things around you look? How do they sound? How do you feel?
5 Ask yourself some key questions. Does your goal fit with your other plans in your life? If you were successful would this cause conflict with anyone around you? What obstacles stand in your way?
6 List action steps you need to take. You should have at least eight or ten steps and an estimation of how long each will take.
7 Review your goals frequently.

Team building skills

Though the pace of change makes fortune telling difficult, the following trends with regard to teams are here to stay:

- pressures to meet competition and create a more democratic workplace will lead to more and more teamworking

- as the traditional, hierarchical organization disappears and companies reorganize themselves around processes the need for teams will increase

- permanent teams will be replaced by temporary, cross-functional teams that come together to work on projects or tasks

- the number of managers will continue to decline and those who remain will become coaches or facilitators

- social changes will support organizational change as education systems produce more team players rather than stars.

147

What you need to do to survive and ride these changes is to discover the secrets of forming, serving on and leading a highly-productive team. In their book *'The Wisdom of Teams'*[1] Katzenbach and Smith define a team as 'a small number of people with complementary skills who are committed to a common purpose, performance goals and approach for which they hold themselves mutually accountable'.

This definition highlights six elements that support the developments of teams and encourage superior work performance. These are:

1 **Small Numbers** – according to McKinsey, the management consultants, most successful teams have two to twenty-five members, and the majority have fewer than ten.

2 **Complementary Skills** – Katzenbach and Smith maintain that a team cannot succeed unless they contain three types of complementary skills and knowledge:

[1] Manard Business School Press (1993).

- technical or functional expertise

- problem solving and decision making skills

- interpersonal skills.

3 **Assortment of styles** – you will remember from chapter 4 the importance of different decision making styles and the different team roles as highlighted by Belbin to ensure that you have a wide enough repertoire within the team.

4 **Common purpose and performance goals** – a team's immediate goals must be in line with its overall purpose, otherwise team members will get confused and discouraged.

5 **A common approach** – teams need time to develop their working approach. The members should assign themselves specific tasks, stick to schedules, identify development needs and plan ways to make and change decisions.

6 **Mutual accountability** – a group becomes a team only when it can hold itself collectively accountable. Shared work towards common objectives eventually breeds trust within the group.

148

All teams go through a difficult formative process that culminates in an optional level of productivity, quality and decision making. To help your team succeed, you must understand and appreciate the different phases in the development of that team. You must help guide your team through these difficult stages of struggle and adaptation toward the final stage.

Forming is the first stage of a team, a time when the different parts of the team have been brought together and charged with a task. People are unsure of their roles and the roles of others. They question who has the power, who the abilities. They may have prejudices or misconceptions about team mates. All this creates an atmosphere of uneasiness.

To help this team progress you must:

- reassure members the reasons why they were asked to be on the team

- confirm individual responsibilities that come with membership

- acquaint team members with each other.

Storming is the painful but necessary second formative phase. In this phase, the team works out its jobs, its roles, the relationships in the team, the nature of potential barriers, and infrastructure support. During this phase, different personalities, different agendas and different backgrounds will lead to conflict about goals and roles. These conflicts have to be resolved before any work can be accomplished. Your role here is essential. You cannot leave the team to its own devices to sort out the conflicts.

You must:

■ explain limits

■ offer suggestions

■ facilitate the resolution of conflict.

In most teams, three fifths of the time is spent in the first two stages. Some teams never emerge from the storming phase.

Norming occurs after individuals on the team have struggled through and roles have emerged. They are less defensive and more interested in moving forward with other team members to find solutions. Now is your time to become coach and facilitator.

Performing stage is reached when the synergies of the team are operating at full capacity.

A team is a gathering of people. To make it work effectively, you must inspire that group of people towards creative and innovative action. For this reason the best team leaders are often infectious self-starters. They are active, energetic, and excited about the task. Don't confuse energy and excitement with aggressiveness and noise. Quiet leaders are just as effective, if not more so than back slapping, loud mouths. Show that you are involved and concerned. Be present and active, but also be prepared to listen.

Some important roles for you as a team leader are as follows:

1 To bring perspective – ie to help others understand the larger issues at stake. A broader perspective helps a team perceive different possible paths towards its goals.

2 To help the team work across functional boundaries, encour-

aging co-operative action where none had existed before.

3 Help the team set clear believable goals based on vision. Teams often fail because team members:

- don't believe in the outcome
- don't believe the outcome is reachable
- cannot work out what the boss really wants as an outcome.

4 Help your team define clearly the role of each member. The issue is not one of assigning tasks, but rather of clarifying responsibilities.

5 Remember that you and the rest of your team have different communication styles and learning styles (remember chapter 4) and try to adapt your approach. However, don't try to be a chameleon changing with every person's personality. Just remember what type of person you are talking to.

6 Remember hidden agendas which, positive or negative, influence the work of individuals on the team. Unattended, they can eventually undermine the team. You must make an effort to acknowledge and understand the hidden agendas of others as a first step forward to finding satisfactory solutions for both individuals and the team.

In their book 'Why Teams Don't Work'[1], Harvey Robbins and Michael Finby pose some basic rules that can help your teams accept and even enhance the change process.

1 **Plans for change** – encourage the team to plan how the change should happen, to what time schedule, with which participants.

2 **They must have ownership of the change** – they should have a hand in deciding where the change will take the team.

3 **Communicate** – share information with the team.

4 **Create a positive expectation** – the team will support change if the positive results of the change are clearly explained.

5 **Create support/influence networks** – external networks reassure the team and champion the team to others.

[1] Petersons/Paceselles Books, Princeton NJ (1995).

6 **Generate critical mass** – ie it should include a sufficient number of advocates, champions and outside friends.

7 **Follow through and follow up** – keep on top of your team during the change process but don't police. Coach them through the barriers.

8 **Allow mistakes to be made** – don't punish a team that takes risks because you want it to search continuously for innovation and improvement.

9 **Keep the techniques simple.**

10 **Lead** – help to draw up the vision. Create expectations and then keep the team motivated with ongoing support.

Being an effective leader

In chapter 4 we introduced you to the concept of the Leader's Window, which was highlighted by John Beck and Neil Yeager in their book, *'The Leader's Window'*[1]. From their research they identified that the best leaders use all four leadership styles in the 1-4-3-2 sequence. They call this the empowerment cycle. This means that while they delegate as much responsibility as they can they start out with a clear direction to help people get started. They expect their staff to want information, explanations, and a full understanding of what results must be achieved, then to encourage teams to work together and take responsibility, they delegate. Next, if they are good leaders, they ask questions and listen so they have an understanding of the problems and opportunities experienced so that they can help staff move forward. Finally, if they feel they need to take action, they accept input and make timely decisions.

151

There is no doubt in today's high-involvement environment that to be an effective leader you must be able to empower staff. So if this role is not your natural leadership style how can you develop it?

Micha Popper and Raanan Lipshutz in their article, *'Putting Leadership Theory to Work'*,[2] identified three components of successful leadership:

[1] John Wiley & Sons, New York (1994).
[2] Leadership and Organization Development Journal Vol., 14, No 7, 1993, pp. 23-27.

1 Self efficacy – ie the extent to which a person believes that they can perform well in a specific domain.

2 Developing awareness of modes of motivating others.

3 Developing specific skills (eg giving feedback).

The development of specific skills to be a change winner we are covering in this chapter. The development of ways of motivating others we discuss in the chapter on empowerment. The difficult part is how do you develop self efficacy? Popper and Lipshutz suggest that their studies of great coaches provide a set of basic principles for developing self efficacy. These can be described as follows:

1 **Learn from a mentor.** Imitate or identify with someone whom you perceive to be good at motivating people.

2 **Role learning.** Identify what you think is a competent performance of an effective leader and then deliberately copy that performance. Unlike learning from a mentor, this is based on your rational choice of what is most suitable for you and your circumstances.

3 **Learn through doing.** Try out new ways of doing things and learn from the success or failure of your own actions.

4 **Learn by validation.** Learning by comparing your views of effective leadership with others at workshops, lectures, meetings, etc.

5 **Learn through concepts**. Learn through exposure to new novel approaches presented by successful experts.

6 **Personal growth.** Get feedback constantly on your performance and try to change and improve as a result of this.

These approaches are not either/ors but should all be pursued in tandem. It is only by doing this that you really will start to believe that you can perform well using a style with which you were not previously comfortable. You will have already covered the more general aspects of learning in chapter 3.

Risk taking

■ ■ ■

In today's environment of continuous change the change winner is going to confront situations they have not had to deal with before. They are therefore going to be placed in a position where they are going to take risks. However, these risks must be calculated, ie the likelihood of success must be greater than that of failure.

There are three key stages in the process of assessing and controlling risks in any environment:

- identifying hazards (the potential causes of damage)

- assessing risks (the likelihood of failure occurring and its severity)

- designing, implementing and monitoring measures to eliminate or minimize risk.

Those who take unnecessary risks without carrying out this type of assessment are unnecessarily dangerous and you should not seek to emulate them.

153

Coaching skills

In the chapter on empowerment we discuss the role of the manager becoming more that of a coach or facilitator. However, even if you decide that empowerment is not the route of your organization coaching skills are invaluable in today's changing organizations. The aim of coaching in a business sense is to review and challenge old values, attitudes, styles of dealing with people and strategies for getting

Coaching skills are invaluable in today's changing organizations.

things done, so that people can work more effectively and maintain high-performance levels. In the broadest sense, the aim of the coach is to empower the member of staff by increasing their understanding, sense of direction and purpose so that they can find a more stimulating and fulfilling way of working in which they can maximize their contribution to the business.

Many staff have the technical skills and knowledge to do the job but they often lack the non-technical skills. These skills involve managing relationships, understanding one's own impact, focusing on key work and approaching problem solving in less rigid ways.

Linda Marsh in her article, *'Good Manager: Good Coach?'*[1], concludes that good coaching has six dimensions:

1 Being open to ideas, enabling the learner to participate and make his/her own decisions and mistakes.

2 Creating a good atmosphere and being supportive.

3 Giving specific feedback, balancing praise and criticism.

4 Demonstrating personal interest and involvement.

5 Setting clear targets.

6 Ensuring thorough preparation and risk assessment before doing something different.

She also discovered that there was a high correlation between those managers incorporating these dimensions into their management style and the performance and motivation of those people working for them. High achieving and highly-motivated teams and individuals are essential for the survival of organizations in today's environment so as a potential change winner you should endeavour to incorporate as many of these dimensions into your own management style as possible.

Encouraging creativity

Creativity is becoming increasingly popular in management circles. With a more fashion-orientated marketplace there is a greater need for more innovative products so higher levels of creativity are essential. Another reason is that it is believed that eventually technology will take over most of the clerical functions of management, but the one function which they may never be able to replace completely is that of the human mind. The role of manager could therefore become more one of engendering and facilitating creativity in others.

We can define creativity as the process of human thought that leads to new ideas. The real art of successful creativity in organizations is in ensuring that ideas are both appropriate and applicable to organizational needs.

[1] Industrial and Commercial Training, Vol. 24, No 9, 1992, pp. 3–8.

A useful model of creativity developed by Perkins, a psychologist at Harvard University is the, 'Snowflake,' model.[1]

Perkins determined that there are six different psychological traits found among creative people:

- objectivity and the encouragement of criticism

- mental mobility

- a high tolerance to complexity

- inner motivation – a zealous passion for work

- excellent at problem finding and problem solving

- an enjoyment of risk taking.

He found that while a creative person may not have all six of these traits the more a person has the more creative he or she tends to be. You will note that a number of these traits are common with that of the change winner.

What then are the implications of encouraging creativity both in yourself and in others?

Firstly, you need to raise awareness and interest people in the concept of creativity. Then the essential ingredient in encouraging creativity is giving people the opportunity to develop and try out original ideas in a secure environment. One way of doing this is to use creative circles. For creativity to be successful, staff must be allowed the freedom to make mistakes. The surest way to stifle enthusiasm is to create an atmosphere of, 'You must be right – always!'

Majaro proposed a multidisciplinary, multifunctional, multi-level team, ie a creative circle for establishing an ideas flow within the organization.[2]

A creative circle runs on much the same lines as Quality circles in that it provides individuals from all sections of the organization with a way to discuss new ideas and innovations in a secure environment.

[1] 'The Mind's Best Work', Perkins, D., Harvard University Press, Cambridge, MA, (1981).
[2] 'The Creative Gap', Majaro, S., Longman, London, (1988).

You can obtain many new thoughts and approaches this way, but while having ideas is easy, getting ideas that strategically fit both the organization and the external environment is more difficult. You may want to set in place a framework that will allow individuals in the creativity circle to push innovative ideas through a filtering system. The filter system might consist of matches against the following:

- **external environment** – political, social, economic, technical and environmental aspects, opportunities and threats

- **internal environment** – physical resources available, finances, people, structure, policy, strengths and weaknesses both actual and perceived

- **time scale** – for final approval and the most appropriate time for new approaches to be introduced and the communication of changes.

156

As with all the skills outlined in the chapter, this one approach alone will not lead to success but should be used as one of a battery.

Project management skills

Change as you are only too aware by now is difficult in most circumstances, but is particularly challenging in large mature firms with strong functional groups, extensive specialization, large numbers of people and multiple, on-going, operating pressures. You will need project management skills to a greater or lesser degree depending on the complexity of your organization.

Kim B Clark and Steve C Wheelwright in their article, *'Organizing and Leading "Heavyweight" Development Teams,'*[1], draws up the different profile for a lightweight or heavyweight project manager. You will need to decide which is the most appropriate to your organization. However, the more internally focused, centralized, more mature, hierarchical, functional and less involving of its workforce the more your project approach will need to be towards the heavyweight end.

[1] California Management Review, Spring, (1992).

Project Manager Profile

Factor	Heavy-weight				Light-weight
	Very	Moder-ate	Neutral	Moder-ate	Very
	5	4	3	2	1
Span of co-ordination response					
Duration of responses					
Responsible for specs, cost, layout, components					
Working level contact with front-line workers					
Direct contact with customers					
Multilingual/multidisciplined skills					
Role in conflict resolution					
Marketing imagination/concept champion					
Influence in specialist functions, eg marketing					
Total score					

157

A heavyweight project manager will lead, evaluate other members of the core team, and is the person to whom the team will report throughout the project duration. The lightweight project manager will see themselves as either neutral or a facilitator with regard to problem solving, whereas the heavyweight project manager sees themselves as championing the project. They make sure that those who work on the project understand the concept and are out there amongst the 'troops' ensuring that decisions are made and implemented whenever and wherever needed.

Referring back to the Leadership window in chapter 4 the heavyweight project manager is using the leadership Style in S1 (high direction) to S2 (high direction and high support), whereas the lightweight project manager is operating in the S3 (high support) to S4 (low direction and low support) quadrants. However, you must remember that as with the leadership styles discussed in the Leadership Window you must be prepared to change as staff become more empowered and are ready to take concepts forward on their own. The key to being a change winner is flexibility. So do not try to find the holy grail equivalent of management style, but aim to understand the facets of leadership style so that you can change and select them as you would your own clothes depending on the prevailing climate.

Self improvement and career management skills

The delayering that results from most change initiatives today has reinforced the fact that no organization today is able to offer any individual a job for life, still less a job with regular promotion up the hierarchy. Yet for many of us that is what career development has led us to expect. The psychological contract between us and our organization has changed. It used to run something like: 'I give you loyalty, compliance and functional expertise, and you give me security, regular promotions, salary increases and care in times of trouble.'

Yet by downsizing, outsourcing and delayering, many organizations have had to renege on this deal. Instead they offer constant challenge and they reward only those employees who are eager to meet it. In exchange they expect flexibility, responsibility, accountability and long working hours.

Unfortunately people are having difficulty making this transition. Roffey Park Management Institute in its current work among over 200 public and private sector organizations has found that as few as 1 per cent of employers within a flatter structure are showing the behaviour and characteristics that will make that structure work. The old habits, work patterns, people and bureaucracy are trying to re-emerge. In order to survive, these organizations will have to get rid of these people or build upon a new psychological contract with these people that offers employees the opportunity to develop themselves and increase their employability in return for the increased skills and output required of them under a flat structure.

How can you go about negotiating one of these new style contracts and ensure that you develop yourself into a change winner? The main way is by thinking about your job more strategically. You need to recognize your job flexibility and your own choices in the job.

Nanette Fondas and Rosemary Stewart in their article, *'How managers can think strategically about their Jobs'*[1], found that by viewing their jobs more strategically, managers have different lines of action open to them by reviewing:

1 How they divide their time between people in their networks.

2 Where they focus their attention most often and,

3 Where they try to have an impact.

Listed below are the things that you need to do to ensure that you develop yourself not only for the job you have today but the ones you want in the future, which you will need to find for yourself.

1 Recognise the job's flexibility.

Job descriptions no longer rigidly define a manager's domain and there is less emphasis on them in the rapidly changing world of today. You are expected to contribute more broadly. This gives you the opportunity to enhance not only your own but your organization's effectiveness. Go on show what a star you can be.

You also have to work across more boundaries than before. This gives you more freedom to interpret the job in a personal way and to develop and practise new skills in new areas.

2 Learn to differentiate between the demands and choices in your job.

Management choices

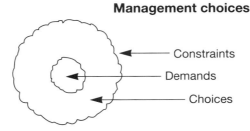

Source: Fondas and Stewart, 'How Managers Can Think Strategically about their Jobs.'

[1] *Journal of Management Development,* Vol. 11, No 7, pp. 10–17

In the diagram the core of a manager's work is labelled 'demands' – the aspects of a job which anyone in it would have to do. Apart from these, you, the manager, have a great deal of choice about what to do, although you may be limited by resource constraints, company policies, technology, employees skills, etc.

It is in this choice area that your added value lies and where you can carve out the role that you desire.

3 Remember that jobs are dynamic in that they change over time.

You need to be constantly asking yourself the following sorts of questions:

- what changes are out their in the environment that could affect the demands and constraints of my post?

- what demands and constraints have diminished or disappeared?

- what new ones are emerging?

- which demands and constraints can I influence to my advantage?

- how do new demands and/or constraints affect what I want to do in this job.

You need to constantly re-evaluate your desires and see whether they are the most appropriate in the light of new solutions.

4 Highlight who is most important to you in achieving your objectives.

Then assess how much time you spend with them. For example, if team building with peers in another department is essential to achieve a primary objective, how much time do you actually devote to it? Keep a diary or review appointments book to check that the reality is the same as your perceptions.

5 Check your networks.

You need contacts both up and down the organization and inside and outside the organization. Networks are especially important today for managers in flexible, dynamic jobs that require you to call upon new people to get things done. You need continually to build and develop your networks both to your current job and also to find your next job (see section on networking).

6 Do not immerse yourself just in the present.

Ensure that you do not concentrate only on short-term goals, but give time and effort on medium and long-term goals as well. Check which choice you are actually making, as distinct from what you believe you make, by first making a list of the actions needed to work towards each of these goals. Then keep a diary for a week or more to track the different activities and the amount of time devoted to each. You must differentiate between the urgent but unimportant versus the important but not urgent.

7 In which area of the job are you trying to make an impact?

Do you merely try to make an impact in your own unit/department or do you consider what can be done to help the larger organization and get yourself both learning and experienced, and *noticed*.

The most important thing that you need to note is that the psychological contract is now different in that you will give the organization the increased skills and output they require as long as they give you the opportunity to develop yourself. To do this you must think of your job in the strategic context – as a learning opportunity – as one step on a pathway which you are now laying for yourself.

Your future is in your own hands

You can no longer rely on the organization to reward you with a secure career path. We have outlined to you the skills that we believe you need to win at change. We have given you some ideas on how to manage your career strategically. Now is the time to put the two together. Look at your current job. See where the development opportunities are – make sure you take advantage of them. Re-evaluate your choices but remember that once you can no longer find development opportunities you must consider other options. We will help you draw up a personal action plan in chapter 11.

The best response to the power of others is to identify areas of common interest and actively seek to achieve these goals

10

$$\blacksquare \quad \blacksquare \quad \blacksquare$$

Influencing the
direction of change

**Understanding conflict · managing conflict · assessing your
power base · using power · winning over stakeholders ·
evaluating the forces for and against change
· sustaining change**

Many organizational initiatives fail because of a lack of understanding how power operates within their corporate walls. Instead chief executives blame the approach being implemented. History repeats itself when the next wonder business idea fails to take root for the same reason. This chapter tells you how to manage conflict and use the leaders of power to influence the key stakeholders. It also shows you how to prevent the organization from slowly and surreptitiously returning to its old ways by explaining the many other factors that you need to influence. Organizations that ignore these issues are like sponges. They absorb change only quietly to reinstate themselves when the pressure for change is dissipated. This is why their cynics gleefully point out that the new initiative will fail as surely as the ones before it.

Understanding conflict
■ ■ ■

Conflict can help you to clarify your thinking and to test out the robustness of your arguments. It can also be a creative force, suggesting different ways of seeing and doing. You can also resolve problems at an early stage when they can cause least damage. This is because those who argue against you spell out their reservations, usually with great clarity. Conflict energizes discussions and can add to the momentum of change, if handled successfully. You can use conflict to create an unbreakable team spirit. You can achieve this by uniting against an 'enemy' such as a competitor.

Conflict avoids dangerous over-optimism. It guards against failing to understand the underlying issues. This can happen when colleagues are unwilling or unable to express different views. This can take the form of 'group think' when each member of the group reinforces the increasingly unrealistic views of their colleagues. This can happen when leaders build teams with too many like-minded people. You may well recognize this problem not only in politics but also in some of the organizations in which you have worked. The surest way to avoid this is to value diversity and seek it out in your recruitment strategies.

Conflict can be found in most organizations, though there may be a reluctance to acknowledge it. After all, it goes against cohesive approaches such as corporate vision and organization wide goals that are growing in popularity. You need to understand conflict so that you tackle the causes and not the symptoms of conflict. A frequent source of conflict is the difference between the interests of the groups and individuals within organizations. This can be between departments fighting for resources, between one level of staff and another over rewards. Some conflict is based, however, not on substantive issues but personality clashes and misunderstandings due to poor communication. The fear of change, that one party will gain an advantage over another often results in substantive conflict. You will certainly recognize many of the following types of conflict:

Resource conflict happens when money or other resources are scarce and each party feels that their slice of the cake is too small. This sounds very familiar. It could take place about pay, the size of company car or office space. In some organizations, there is much conflict and competition about whether you have the newest and most powerful microcomputer on your desk or the best notebook computer in your briefcase.

Functional conflict takes place in organizations where the different departments work in isolation. Each has its own agenda and priorities that rarely coincide with each other. For instance sales staff may offer large discounts at the end of the year so that they can exceed their sales targets. This does not benefit the organization as a whole. Many of the sales would have been made anyway. The price cutting brings these orders forward so that sales may fall dramatically when prices are raised back to their previous levels. This pattern of boom and slump creates serious problems for production. They may be forced into using expensive overtime one month and be faced with idle capacity the next. This is a recipe for warfare between the functions.

Value conflict can occur between different cultures and personality types who may be in separate functions. Finance staff may restrain marketing staff from implementing their bold plans. They may well be seen as an 'over-cautious bunch of bean counters' for their pains. The finance view of marketing may be that they are reckless 'wide boys and girls.'

Hierarchical conflict occurs between different levels of the organization. Often, the upper tier seeks to increase its control by asking for more information from the lower level. The latter resent what they see as undue interference from above that distracts them from their main tasks. The top tier says of the other, 'they are out of control' and the other responds with 'they treat us like puppets.'

Staff-line conflict is a feature of organizations with powerful head offices. Staff functions often combine an advisory role with more directive policy and monitoring functions. This type of conflict can be voiced as the 'out of touch bureaucrats from the Kremlin' versus 'the shambling amateurs from the sticks.' Many organizations have reduced this type of conflict by devolving more responsibilities to the line. Typically, personnel has passed recruitment down to line mangers.

Role conflict can reduce staff performance when their managers place conflicting demands on them. Customer facing staff can be put in the invidious position of having to increase their client contacts while improving their standard of service. This can make life very difficult for the staff concerned and can result in high staff turnover.

Personality conflict is the most unhelpful of all. It usually damages all the parties involved without producing any benefits. This makes it a classic example of lose-lose conflicts. If you are involved in a personality conflict, try to find at least a couple of redeeming features in the other person. This will halt the downward spiral and may well lead to an improvement in your relationship.

The real reasons for conflict are often concealed behind much more acceptable ones. Thus those who oppose change may invoke customers in their arguments. They might claim that

customers are happy with things as they are. The true causes
are more likely to be the fear of losing staff, influence, status and
perhaps a job! However, they are unlikely to win wider support
if they make this explicit. So be careful to discriminate between
stated conflict and hidden conflict. Much time and effort can be
wasted on stated conflict that would be better spent on resolving
hidden conflict.

Managing conflict

Conflict is too easily seen as good or bad. In reality, it can be
quite rational and predictable as it is often caused by the diver-
gent interest and objectives of those involved. The key factor is
not conflict itself but how people respond to it. Some action orientated people do not care about conflict or its consequences.
They just want to push ahead with change as quickly as possible. Their aim is to defeat their opponents as decisively as possible. This will turn into a win-lose type of conflict where the
winner takes all or as much as possible. You might even achieve
your victory. However, the price could be very high. The losers
may be hell bent on gaining revenge. They may plot and scheme
and wait for your moment of weakness and exploit it to the full.
They could conduct low intensity, guerrilla warfare. This is very
difficult to counteract and can frustrate your aims without
putting the guerrillas at serious risk to themselves. Taken to an
extreme, this can become a lose-lose conflict where humiliating
and defeating the opponent becomes an end in itself. The original reason for the conflict becomes lost in history.

Another response to conflict is to avoid it with great skill. On
occasions, this is a good strategy as you have neither the time
nor resources to become involved in
every conflict. However, if used indis-
criminately, it can lead to paralysis and
confusion. This will also be taken as a
sign of weakness. This response takes the accommodating
behaviour of the diplomats we met in chapter 3 to extremes.

*Change winners seek
for win-win solutions*

These responses to conflict are unlikely to be successful in the
long term. The first step is to have a positive attitude towards
conflict and realize that you need to manage it instead of being

167

driven by it. We will show you how change winners manage conflict effectively. They seek win-win solutions where all parties feel that they have won.

To do this, you need to understand the other party's point of view in great depth. This means that you have to put yourself in their shoes. Make sure that you feedback to them your understanding of any critical points they make. It is very easy to mishear criticism and this approach will help you avoid that problem. Another advantage of this way of relating to criticism is that the critics feel heard and will be more willing to look at things from your point of view. You must seek out the hidden conflict rather than just concentrating on the stated reasons. This can be done by asking the key stakeholders how to:

- improve products for customers

- improve co-operation with suppliers and contractors

- enrich the jobs for staff

- reduce costs and improve quality.

You and your organization will need to trust the other parties with commercially sensitive information so that you all have common understanding of your organization's position. This means both the good and bad news. The other parties will not trust you if you only give them the news that fits your current position.

You will then be in a position to ensure that as many of the key issues on each other's agendas are met as possible. You can ask the participants to come up with creative solutions for seemingly contradictory goals. The other parties may make unrealistic demands for instance, staff might not want to do work they find boring or only work when it suits them. Avoid the temptation to point out that they are impossible to deliver. Rather give the problem back to them. You could say, if you do not want to do particular tasks, how could the process be carried out differently so that the organization achieves the desired outcomes?

Record the decisions made and make sure that all parties have the same understanding. By fully involving the stakeholders they will not only own the process of resolving the conflicts but also implementing the solutions. This approach will also earn trust of all those involved. You need to make sure that you do as you say, otherwise you will lose this hard-earned trust. You will be in a better position to put this into practice once you have worked through the rest of the chapter.

Assessing your power base

Having learnt how to achieve win-win solutions, the next step is to understand the sources of your power and how you can best use them. This will give you much more flexibility and scope to achieve your aims. Each organization has its own structures of power that need to be understood and carefully addressed. Power can fluctuate as is often shown by the demob happy attitude of someone who is working out their notice. All of a sudden, the power of the organization and its managers over that individual is diminished. Periods of sudden change, take-overs, reorganizations, the departure of senior managers can alter the balance of power. Opportunists seize such moments to carve out their next career move.

Reward power

This form of power consists of being able to distribute resources such as promotion, bonus pay, prestigious company cars and opulent offices. To exercise reward power you must have control over the resources that are valued by those whom you wish to influence. The power of union leaders depends on their capacity to 'deliver' what their members want. Bosses who are known to be moving on soon become lame ducks as they lose much of their reward power. They will not be around when their staff's performance pay is assessed or when promotion is being considered.

Organizations dominated by reward power can be obsessed by status symbols. There are fierce squabbles about who will move into the recently vacated large office or about company car envy. Organizations such as firms of head-hunters base their remuneration system on reward power, where consultants are motivated to bill ever higher to get the largest bonus, the company award, etc.

Organizations that use performance related pay seek to use reward power to improve their results. This strengthens the reward power of managers where they are the sole judges of performance. However, staff are also given reward power in organizations where they conduct upwards appraisals of their managers.

Other organizations feel that some sorts of reward prevent all staff from identifying with the organization. They have abolished the canteens for each staff type and reserved parking spaces. Archie Norman, chief executive of Asda, loans the company Jaguar and parking space to the member of staff who comes up with the best ideas for the firm. Thus the reward of the luxury car goes not to position but to those who use their expert knowledge creatively to the organization's benefit.

Position power

170

This is very important in hierarchical organizations with clear structures and grades where someone can place you in the hierarchy from your job title. Its attraction is that you do not necessarily have to earn it through your ability but rather through years of consistent support to the same boss. You hold position power provided you retain your boss's confidence and he keeps his job. Access to networks is often based on position power. This can give the holder a power base in the organization and sometimes outside it.

Managers with a high degree of autonomy, large budgets and many staff are the proud possessors of resource power as well as position power. In some organizations, the head of research and development can have a substantial amount of resource power. On the other hand, jobs with heavy operational pressures that tie up managerial resources with fire fighting limit the scope of position power.

Position power can be lost when a boss excludes a manager from vital information or fails to give them plumb projects they could have reasonably expected to be theirs. Access to vital information culled from negotiations with top management can greatly strengthen trade union representatives in their more routine dealings with middle managers.

Rule based power

There are others who exercise power by drawing up rules and regulations so that they do not have to be present for their wishes to be followed. These documents can still hold force long after their authors are gone. Rule based power requires a stable environment otherwise it will be challenged from below when the rules become out of date. This form of power can also be used by those lower in the organization as a form of negative power to stop something happening. This is the 'more than my job's worth' mentality of bureaucracy where personal agendas are often hidden behind rules and regulations.

Information and power

One of the features of position power is access to information and the capacity to deny it to others. This can be **information from above** that might reveal the financial health of the organization. Plans for contraction or expansion can be useful to furthering the recipient's career, even if it is to jump ship!

Information can also come from across the organization from one function to another, or fail to do so. Addressing the failure in the flow of **lateral information** is at the heart of re-engineering where cross-functional teams replace functional structures. TQM goes some way in this direction as well through the use of teams with a somewhat shorter span.

Many organizations ignore **information from below** at their peril. Front-line staff often know not only the most important problems but also have a good idea how to solve them. They might also be in regular contact with customers and have a good idea how to improve products or services. They are likely to keep this information to themselves when they feel that they are not listened to or are undervalued. Gaining access to information from below is one of the key aspects of TQM.

Managers who can combine information from above, horizontally and below are prized by their bosses as they have a far more complete picture. People who always know what is going on are also greatly valued in networks.

Some of the greatest exponents of information power are civil servants. Their ministers are heavily dependent on them as they change departments so frequently that they are rarely able to develop a knowledge base of their own. Also ministers have so many engagements each day that they have to memorize a 'line to take' that encapsulates the government's position on each issue. Some civil servants have tried to drown new ministers in a sea of paperwork in the hope that they would look to them for rescue. Civil servants can also screen their ministers from information they would rather they did not know. Giving answers that appear to answer the question yet reveal very little is an art form that they devote many years to perfect.

Expert power

Expert power comes from possessing knowledge or skills that are valued by others. Its attraction is that you only have to know a little more than anyone else about a vital topic to be regarded as an expert by that group. It is the form of power that is most easily accepted and readily sought after by others as the growing army of management consultants testifies. Where holders of expert power become unpopular is when they appear not to use their knowledge to help others, exclude people through the use of jargon and patronize people. Rightly or wrongly, this is the image of many managers in information technology. Expert power is subject to the vagaries of fashion. Holders who are unable to update their expertise rapidly will be quickly removed from the corporate shop window.

Charismatic power

Charismatic power can be very seductive. It is very difficult to define. It is some sort of star quality that sets some people apart from others. Charismatic leaders can easily sense the mood of audiences. They start off in step with them and then lead them in their own direction. They are most effective in organizations where beliefs play a large part such as voluntary organizations.

Normative power

Normative power exists where staff share some or all of the values of a particular organization. They tend to refer to their organization as 'we' and 'us'. An example of normative power is nurses working regular unpaid overtime because they feel that this is the only way that they can care for patients. Changes to NHS working practices that fail to address the beliefs behind normative power are unlikely to obtain more than lukewarm support at best and outright hostility at worst. Normative power is an important feature of the voluntary sector.

Informal power

The exclusive gentlemen's clubs, the local squash or golf club can all be sources of informal power. They can be very valuable sources of jobs and project based work to independent professionals. These networks can also provide a useful source of inside track information. Those excluded are at a disadvantage. To women they form some of the toughest panels of the glass ceiling that can restrict their careers. Informal power is frequently kept concealed, particularly when people are in bed with each other! Knowing an embarrassing detail of a boss's record has also furthered the career of some individuals. Informal networks begin at birth for new members of very influential families with well-connected parents, uncles and older siblings. This can be supplemented by public school and Oxbridge. A study of the background of cabinet ministers, civil servants and captains of industry shows that these traditions are still strong. Managers also need to be aware that a member of staff who acts as 'spokesperson' can influence senior management, although their position is probably informal.

Negative power

This is the power to prevent or delay something from happening. It can be very effective as it is easy to underrate this subterranean form of power. Even a very small act or failure to act can have a large impact such as forgetting or delaying passing on a crucial piece of information. It can be difficult to catch the really good practitioners. Many projects are like sensitive plants that will die if they are not well tended. It can be very hard to prove who failed to do their share of watering! Negative power is the response of the disaffected and disenfranchised. It is difficult to think of someone who has absolutely no negative power, given how vulnerable organizations have become with their vast flow of information and the high speed at which they need to operate.

Environmental impact

In large, diverse organizations the functions can develop their own culture with quite different sources of power. Finance staff often use a combination of position and rule based power. Computer and technical staff rely on expert power as does the internal consultant. Line managers can use information from their staff to argue effectively in favour of the status quo. The table below shows the type of power that is most effective in a particular environment.

Relationship between power and environment

Type of environment	Type of power most effective
Command and control	Position power
Dynamic, fluid structures	Expert power
Normative	Charismatic, appeal to core values
Bureaucratic	Rule based power

Power is not exercised in a vacuum and it is necessary to understand how the power bases are likely to shift and what external factors will come into play. When jobs are scarce it is easy for organizations and managers to delude themselves how good they are because very few staff leave. However, it is the environmental impact of the economy that makes it difficult for them to escape. The power of employers weakens when the economy becomes buoyant and disgruntled staff can find jobs elsewhere.

The physical environment can support the development of alliances between those who work in close proximity to each other. Hostility can result when these relationships are broken up to achieve greater efficiency as part of a reorganization. The environment can be used to signal change. Giving the multi-functional project team a base of its own and redecorating working areas when new practices are introduced can be positive reinforcers of change.

The balance between the different types of power has changed over time. There has been an increase in expert power at the expense of position and rule based power in the new flatter organizations. The number and size of command and control organizations have declined as they are being challenged by dynamic ones with fluid structures. The rapid growth of the knowledge based worker is a reflection of the growth role of expert power. It also casts the manager more in the role of the facilitator rather than the technical expert. The span of control of many managers is now so wide it makes it almost impossible for them to be fully conversant of what their expert staff know. The following case study illustrates some of these changes.

175

Conflict between sources of power

THE ENGLAND RUGBY CAPTAIN VERSUS THE ADMINISTRATORS

Position power, expert and normative power crashed head on when the Rugby Union sacked and then reinstated the England captain Will Carling during the 1994/95 season. He was sacked because he called them '57 old farts' in a media interview. He implied that they were a bunch of anachronistic amateurs who were out of tune with a professional world.

Their position power was insufficient to match his expert power. Will Carling also runs a successful leadership training organization. He had the full support of the rest of the team who refused to accept any one else as captain. They all shared the belief that Will Carling was the best man for the job.

The situation parallels the growth of expert power of the stars of delayered organizations where their contribution is large and very visible. Obvious examples are top bond dealers and computer specialists whose expertise represents the organization's main assets. When they walk out the door, their organization is suddenly much poorer. The reward package given to such staff is often larger that of their managers.

Using power

The best response to the power of others is to identify areas of common interest and actively seek to achieve these goals. That way you can begin to develop a useful ally. This can be part of a win-win strategy rather than trying to win at the expense of others. The value of this approach is that you do not have to be in complete agreement with the other party as long as you share enough common goals. In fact agreeing where you differ actually strengthens this type of relationship as you both feel more secure knowing where you each stand. This is why it is essential that your negotiating skills are up to scratch.

Highly-effective power players do not flaunt their power but use it subtly instead. Those who show off their power are despised rather like the nouveau riche. If they throw their weight around too much they are considered bullies. Relying too heavily on reward power can give the recipients the feeling that they are being bought off. If this happens, they may well take what is offered to them but only respond grudgingly in return. They might curtail unrewarded activities and only concentrate on those that are rewarded. Overdoing expert power can be a bore and spouting the rules once too often is the hallmark of the bureaucrat.

What type of power do you have and how can you increase it?

Complete the table below to assess how much power you have. You will do really well to score very high in more than a couple of categories so do not be put off if you do not achieve a high score.

Type of power	Level				
	Very high	**High**	**Moderate**	**Low**	**Very little**
Position power					
Reward power					
Rule based power					
Information from above					

Lateral information					
Information from below					
Expert power					
Charismatic power					
Normative power					
Negative power					

You might be able to increase your position power by becoming a manager of a crucial project and reporting to a board member. If you achieve this you could try to enhance your resource power by seeking to increase your budget or by having more staff assigned to you. Improving your supply of information can be achieved by gaining trust through offering information exchange. What information could you pass on that would be of interest to the others without putting your own position at risk? Offer some information first while keeping some in reserve to reward those who have been generous to you. People who pump others for information without supplying any in exchange are despised for committing an information smash and grab raid. Increasing expert power takes time as with any form of learning, (see chapter 3). Normative power depends on working with the values of those you wish to influence. How do your sets of values compare? Negative power is only to be used in extremis. After all, it is of little interest if you are winning. Trying to increase charismatic power is something many of us failed to achieve as teenagers; it is not even worth thinking about repeating the exercise later in life.

177

Winning over stakeholders

Whatever activity you are involved in that affects the status quo will produce a response amongst the stakeholders. This needs to be carefully monitored as they can sabotage your project by putting up opposition. If they are really pivotal, they can hamper progress by merely being insufficiently committed. They do not have to express outright opposition. The level of involvement you require will also vary according to the type of project. However, if your chief executive does anything less than helping it happen, your chances of success are remote. There is little point progressing the project until his or her commitment is at the required level. The table below shows the key players and their current and desired position. You will need to draw up your own listing of those whom you need to influence for your change initiative to succeed.

Planning stakeholder commitment

Key players	Opposition	No commitment	Let it happen	Help it happen	Make it happen
Chief Executive				xo	
Middle managers		x			o
Junior staff		x			o
Trade unions	x		o		
Shareholders			xo		
Customers		x	o		
Suppliers		x			o

Key: x – position at start
o – position at finish

The forces for and against change

Your next step is to identify those issues that you need to address to increase the commitment to the required level. You can achieve this by force field analysis. You need to strengthen the factors pushing for change while reducing the forces against change. The latter are much harder to influence which is why they tend to be neglected. This can have fatal consequences as the negative forces can strengthen as a reaction to an increase in the factors for change. For instance, if concerns about the limited resources to implement change go unattended, staff will not become involved as they feel that management lack commitment themselves. The table below is drawn up for a TQM project. You need to list the forces at play for your own project with an action plan of how you will influence them.

Evaluating the forces for and against change

For	Against
Fear of loss of sales and jobs	Failure of previous change initiatives
Increase in training	Lack of long-term perspective
Greater worker empowerment	Role of middle managers threatened
Staff want to take more pride in their work	Limited resources to implement change
Staff keen to tackle hassle factors	Feeling that quality is more costly

Sustaining change

The reason why many changes are unsustainable is that they fail to influence all facets of the organization. The diagram below comes from the management consultants McKinsey and shows seven key factors that are interlinked and self reinforcing.

179

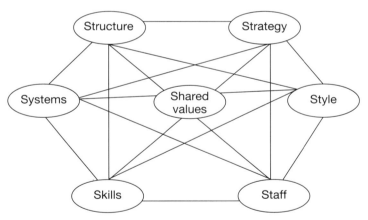

Source: Robert H. Waterman 'The Seven Elements of Strategic Fit', The Journal of Business Strategy, Vol 2, No. 3 (winter 1982) p. 15.

Shared values should not be assumed and taken for granted. The best way to nurture them is to involve staff, suppliers and other key stakeholders in visioning exercises. Staff also need to understand why their contribution is important and their role is valued by senior managers. Staff attitude surveys can be used to monitor progress periodically.

The importance of **strategy** was shown in each of the sections dealing with implementing a specific approach to change and also with addressing stakeholders in this chapter.

Changing **systems** is central to re-engineering with its basis on radically improving processes and in using IT to support much wider spans of activities within one job.

Flattening **structures** is a feature of empowerment and re-engineering and to a lesser extent of TQM. Redesigning structures so that multifunctional teams replace functional structures is central to re-engineering.

Altering management **style** is needed to support change. For instance to make empowerment work the emphasis needs to change from punishing wrong doers to encouraging risk taking. Managers developing the role of coach and internal consultant are other major changes in style.

180

Change strategies require improvements in existing **skills** and developing new ones. Some will argue that this is the most important area of all in achieving and sustaining a competitive advantage.

The level of commitment from **staff** needs to be very high to make empowerment and TQM work. They need to believe in what they do rather than complying with management expectations. You should review your recruitment policy to ensure that new recruits are in tune with your new organization.

Use the table below to set out where you are now and what you want to achieve against each of the key factors.

Changing key factors of your organization

Key factors	What are they now?	What do you want them to be?
Shared values		
Strategy		
Systems		
Structures		
Style		
Skill		
Staff		

Change is inevitable but there are certain strategies that can help you through it.

11

...

Winning at change – a personal action

By this stage in the book you should have a pretty good idea of your own strengths and weaknesses, the position of your own organization, the type of change initiative likely to succeed in its current culture and environment, the skills you need to acquire to master change and how you can influence its direction. At this stage we are determined that you do not now think that the book was all very interesting but that winning at change is far too difficult and that your next purchase at the railway station will be a comfortable fantasy inducing novel. We now want to help you produce your own personal action plan for winning at change.

Biography work
■ ■ ■

You will hopefully remember that back in chapter 4 we stated that 'realization is the first step in personal development' and we advocated that you assess yourself against the profile of change winners. However two of the aspects of change winners that we only explored in the organizational context were self image and the level of self knowledge.

Rennie Fritchie in her article, *'Biography Work – the missing part of Career Development'*[1], makes the point that action planning in the career development sense can only take place against the biographical details of what people want overall in their lives, based on their past experiences and their future aspirations.

In her work in career development Fritchie has developed a framework of two fundamental questions and seven strategies. We would advise from our own experience of working through this framework in workshops facilitated by Rennie that before you draw up your particular action plan, you work through the framework so that your action plan for winning at change fits into your overall life plan.

[1] Industrial and Commercial Training Journal Vol. 22, No 2, 1990, pp 27–31.

Fundamental Questions

1 What kind of human being do you want to be?

Here you should describe the kinds of skills, abilities, qualities, disposition, character and understanding that you want to have as a human being. Do not fall into the trap of describing what you think others want you to be. (Describe your real sense of self.) Imagine yourself sitting on a park bench aged 70, what would you remember of your life with pleasure. This may point to items that appear to be essential now but will emerge as trivial over time.

2 What do you want to do with your life?

Think in large as well as small ways of achievements, actions and important issues. As you have thought about the sort of person you want to be, now you need to consider how this fits into the wider world – with your family, your career, society, etc. What very particular contribution do you wish to make?

185

These answers can then act as guiding stars in a life faced with many choices and give you two personal and basic points at all times. It means when you see the opportunity for change or development you can test this against your two guiding stars to see if it takes you where you really want to go.

Strategy questions

1 Where are you?

Describe here your current life stage, both in a personal and career sense. This should give you a comprehensive and realistic picture of where you are.

2 How did you get here?

Here you should look backward in your life and trace all the elements, happenings, and people who have influenced your life so far. It should include positives and negatives.

3 Where do you want to go?

Use the information from 1 and 2 and begin to describe your

immediate real intentions. Which choices, actions, values, and behaviour will move you from where you are now towards your desired ideal. You must focus on attainable and measurable goals.

4 How will you get there?

Look at what helped and what hindered you in your journey so far, but also consider new ways of making things happen which are in line with your hopes, values and aspirations.

5 What will you do when you arrive?

What will it feel like? How can you sustain and enjoy the situation and continue to grow and benefit and move on to the next goals?

6 Where to next?

186

Life is a continuous process so you must look beyond your immediate horizons to gain a sense of perspective and continuity. What are your long-term goals to move you to the kind of human being you want to be and have the life you want.

7 How do you begin?

This is the beginning of the real action plan. Now when you go through the action plan to be a change winner you can do it in the context of your life as a whole, not just in the organizational context.

Eric Olson in his book '*12 Steps to Mastering the Winds of Change*'[1] interviewed a large number of high-achievers and sent surveys to prominent people listed in '*Who's Who in America*' and recorded the results. After analyzing hundreds of interviews and survey results he came to the conclusion that top performers use similar strategies to deal with change. He identifies the twelve steps high-achievers use to take advantage of the one sure thing in their lives and yours **change**. We are going to use these 12 steps to help you prepare your action plan.

[1] Macmillan Inc, New York, 1993.

High achiever skills required
■ ■ ■

Step one: View change as a challenge.

Olson identified that top performers do have some special skills but also have three essential characteristics:

- they were challenged by change rather than stressed and exhausted by it.

- they maintained a sense of control in that they felt they could influence the outcome.

- they were highly committed to and very involved with their jobs.

In order to view change as a challenge you need to understand why change is inevitable and then what you can do to meet the challenge. Re-read chapter 1 and chapter 3 so you can spot the difficulties ahead but know how best to respond.

187

Step two: Build commitment.

High-flyers were found to set effective goals and action plans and then be committed to them.

Ensure that you have set yourself goals. You were asked to do this in the biography section earlier, but also refer to the section on goal setting in chapter 9. Then produce action plans for achieving those goals within a given timetable. Review your goals frequently. Remember that if chapter 4 revealed that you have skills to acquire to win at change, timetable these into your action plan.

Step three: Stay committed.

It is difficult to stay committed when you are beset by setbacks, problems and other challenges. Maintain commitment by:

- persistence – hang on in there.

- searching for alternatives – there must be more than one path to success. Look for people who have been successful – use them as role models.

Remember your mission that you set for yourself at the beginning of this section – you know what sort of person you want to be and the kind of life you want to lead now just work slowly but surely towards it.

Step four: Know when to control, when to let go.

Eighty-nine per cent of those surveyed agreed with the statement 'I exert an important influence on my surroundings'. This belief gives them both power and the resistance to bounce back from the knocks. People who feel powerless act as if they were victims of forces beyond their control. Top achievers have similar ways of gaining control. These include:

- focus on what you can control instead of the obstacles.

- make a plan. Take time each day for this, even if this is disrupted try and return to it.

- keep trying.

- think objectively. You can control how you react to events by changing your thoughts.

Chapter 10, 'Influencing the direction of change', helps you to assess your power base, shows you how you can use power, win over stakeholders and manage conflict. Study this so that you do know when to control and when to let go.

Step five: Deal with feedback.

Here are some ways you can cope with feedback both negative and positive:

- keep faith – check the motives of the people giving feedback. Have faith in yourself that you will get it right in the end.

- learn that feedback makes you stronger. Learn from your mistakes seize opportunities.

- change direction – if you really cannot succeed in that direction then try another. To cling on to the debris of unrealistic goals does not take you anywhere.

Step six: Be optimistic – but do not have blind faith.

There is a difference. Blind faith can lead to your not hearing, seeing or thinking about the negatives, but being optimistic means that you realistically assess the situation but then seek out the few remaining positive elements and build on them.

Remember change winners are flexible. They can adapt their acquired skills to the current environment.

Step seven: Use humour.

This can release tension and put things back into perspective.

Step eight: Learn from mistakes.

They provide important knowledge that helps you succeed eventually. You can only double your success rate, but taking more risks without learning from previous mistakes will undoubtedly lead to failures. Therefore make sure that the risks you are taking are calculated ones.

189

Step nine: Maintain perspective then you can arrange events according to their real importance.

Remember the section in chapter 9 on career management skills. Ensure that you keep the different aspects of your job in perspective and see it as a learning opportunity. Make the most of the choices you have.

Step ten: Get your body in shape.

Your mind cannot work nearly so well if it is imprisoned in an unhealthy body.

Step eleven: Build your confidence.

Acquire the skills outlined in chapter 9 if you do not have them, because mastering skills gives rise to self-confidence and helps you meet your goal. Look at every opportunity to develop these skills via role models, mentoring, secondments, etc.

Step twelve: Communicate and help others.

All top achievers surveyed relied on a support system, which included family, friends, colleagues and acquaintances to help them through good times and bad. A network is a support system – so get out there *networking*.

A word of warning – do draw up action plans but do not over-plan. Robert Fritz in his book, *'Creating'*[1], warns that you should not try to plan everything down to the last detail – rather try them out, adjust them, re-evaluate and then try again.

Neither goals nor action plans should be cast in tablets of stone but must live and evolve as you move through them, learn, evaluate and adjust.

But remember if what you want is to be a change winner then success is in your hands.

Whilst we have written the book so that you can dip in and out at will, to get the most from this section you need to have read all the previous chapters. This section ties the various themes together and helps you build on them to maximum advantage. You have carried out your biographical work. You have discovered the steps that other high-achievers have taken, now we will help you to develop you own strategy to become a change winner, whatever that may mean for you.

From the biography work that you have done, you would have drawn up a vision for your whole life. You now need to convert that overall picture into separate sets of goals, eg personal life goals, career goals, etc. For the purposes of concentrating on winning at change in the organizational context will we focus on career goals. However, these are obviously intrinsically inter-linked with the goals in other areas of your life. You must consider the cross impact at all times. For instance, if you decide that to achieve the skill level that you require you will need to be working eighteen hours a day, seven days a week, this will have a huge impact on any personal life goals ie you will not have time to have more than a maximum of six hours sleep!

* Butterworth-Heinemann, Oxford, (1994).

Setting goals

Studies of successful people show that they set themselves clear, well-thought out goals. They set goals for each day and well into the future. They not only know what they want to achieve, but they see it in glorious colour, play the sound track and feel what it would be like. They can rerun this video during difficult times. They can also think of other similar times when they were successful. This gives them the determination to persevere when others would be disheartened. For change winners, there is no such thing as failure, only feedback. This is how successful sports people think. A tennis player who is serving to save the match will be thinking about his or her best serve.

They will not be thinking, what happens if I hit the ball out of court or what if my opponent hits the ball back so brilliantly I cannot return it? This contrasts with less successful people who start to think of past failures when they experience set backs. Another less obvious failing is a tentative approach that others take for lack of commitment. These people are forever qualifying statements. They seek to, intend, work towards, you get the flavour? Imagine how confident you would be if the pilot

> *For change winners, there is no such thing as failure, only feedback.*

on your flight says that he hopes that you will be landing at your destination. Does this mean you may be very late, diverted elsewhere or worse, not arrive at all?

A key difference is to have a compelling vision of what you want to achieve. It is something that you believe will make a real difference to you. Is your goal somewhat uninspiring or something you feel you ought to do? If it is, after a while it will have the appeal of a warm glass of stale champagne.

So how do you create your own video of success? Look at the sequence when you achieve your goal. What will you be doing who will be with you? Freeze the frame so that you can take in all the details. Hear the sound track. What are you saying to yourself and what are others telling you? Then get in touch with what you will feel like. Will you experience that warm glow of deep satisfaction. What other emotions would you feel?

Your goals must have value for you. You must not be tempted by goals that you feel you should pursue because of other people. You can test this by assuming that all the major influencers in your life no longer exist, would you still want that goal? If the goals are not yours alone, you may not feel sufficiently motivated to achieve them. You may feel somewhat cheated if you do attain them.

In order to make your goals come alive, to solidify them and give shape you need to envisage them. We have set out these questions leaving space for you to write in your answers. We suggest you photocopy the page so that you can use it on a regular basis when you re-evaluate and adjust your goals in the light of experience. It is essential that you do write down your answers. When you do assess your goals you need to be able to review your feelings at the time of writing the goals as well your progress towards them. You need to know that when you attain a goal, does it feel as you imagined it would?

192

If you achieved your goal:

What would it look like?

_____

_____

What would you say to yourself and what would others say to you?

_____

_____

What would it feel like?

_____

_____

What would others notice?

_____

_____

It is always important to check out how others are reacting to that attainment of your goals. Are they having the effect you desire? Or because of other's personal agendas or different value sets, will they impact in a negative way?

What help do you need from others?
eg role models, mentors, networks, family support?

_____

_____

What resources would you need in terms of money and time?
eg if you pay somebody to cut the lawn, clean the house, wash the car, will that free up your time to pursue your goals?

_____

_____

What do you need to learn?
Go back to chapter 4 and look at where your profile is out of line with that of a change winner. Then go to chapter 9 to seek out those skills that you need to master change. Make sure that you build the attainment of these skills into your action plan.

_____

_____

What would you have to give up?
You need to consider carefully in view of your biography work the short-term sacrifices you may need to make to achieve longer-term goals. This is why it is so essential that you continually reassess your goals. Many people find themselves continuing with working patterns that are no longer really necessary, it is just that they have become a habit.

_____

_____

How can you still obtain the benefits of what you need to give up in some different way?

To avoid losing commitment to your goals it is important that where you feel you have made sacrifices you find other ways of satisfying those needs. For example, you may have routinely gone out after work for a quick drink with a regular round of friends and colleagues. However, perhaps you decide that in order to achieve your goal, you need to study three nights a week so you must make sure that you make arrangements to still see those people occasionally. In that way you will not be tempted on a sub-conscious level to compromise your goals. You may feel, if you deprive yourself completely that perhaps you could still achieve your goals by studying only two nights a week – the beginning of the slippery slope.

194

What other goals are related to this one and how would they be affected?
You may find that your goals could be in conflict with each other. You may have decided that you want to stay fit and exercise regularly. However, you have also set yourself the goal of reading, writing articles and networking professionally, then you find that you do not have time for both. You will need to find ways of accommodating both goals. Think laterally about this, there are many ways to exercise and there can be ways of combining this with professional networking.

What do you need to do to start?
Talk to people – particularly those that you would identify as successful role models. Find out how they got started, people are generally well-disposed to sharing their successes. When you have some initial thoughts, share them with a close friend for a reality check. You need to ensure that the friends you choose are those who can accommodate a more successful you.

What are the next milestones on the way?
It is important to check your progress against milestones to ensure that you are still moving forward but do not get hung up on timescales. Also view the milestones or sub-goals as a means to an end not an end in themselves.

_____

_____

Can these goals be achieved in your current organization?
Where do you go if they cannot? Chapter 12 deals with what to do if you want to bail out.

_____

_____

You will discover that with this strategy we have given you an approach to drawing up action plans of setting and achieving goals. By asking the same questions but altering the context you will be able to use this process in a number of different settings. It can be used to draw up an action plan for implementing change in your organization. The following chapter describes this in detail.

Neuro Linguistic Programming

This approach to achieving personal excellence has been developed by observing outstanding performers. The field of study is called Neuro Linguistic Programming (NLP). It has a lot to offer otherwise it would have never succeeded with such an uninviting name!

Further reading:

NLP at Work: the difference that makes the difference in business, Sue Knight, Nicholas Brealey, (1995)

There is no doubt that if you are a change winner in a change-losing organization, then you must consider your options

12
∎ ∎ ∎

What if you want to choose to bail out?

**Change winners in a change-losing organization ·
uncomfortable with the type of change in your organization? ·
change lover seeking exciting possibilities · change losers**

Change winners in a change-losing organization
■ ■ ■

If you have scored well against the criteria of a change winner or believe that with effort you can acquire those skills then it is really good news. A word of caution, however. What do you do if you are a change winner in a change-losing organization? These organizations can exhibit many different features. Is your organization one that wants to change but has a history of failed initiatives? Is it like an oil tanker approaching a submerged obstacle but does not realize the obstacle is there until it is too late to

> *Technological change is the wild card and can decimate even the most efficient organization.*

manoeuvre away? Or is it a ship that forgets to post lookouts or posts them but ignores their information because the captain is so supremely confident that he is on the right course? Or could your ship be rendered obsolete by the invention of amphibious cars, lorries and coaches? Remember that technological change is the wild card and can decimate even the most efficient organization.

Whatever the reason, there is no doubt that if you are a change winner in a change-losing organization, then you must consider your options. You may decide that with your considerable skills as a change winner that you can influence the major stakeholders, muster enough resources and take on the challenge of change against the odds. If you succeed, you will definitely deserve the title of 'change winner extraordinaire'. If you fail, nobody will remember that you were a change winner but will tar you with same brush as your organization. However, change winners take calculated risks. You need to go back to chapter 7 and look at the skills involved in risk taking so that you can assess the degree of risk involved in not bailing out.

What if you do decide to bail out? What options are available to you? What aspects of change do you enjoy? You are not looking for a major change in career direction but you are looking for the environment where your flourishing change skills can develop and grow. How do you go about finding this? If you remember in chapters 7 and 11 we described to you the importance of networking. This skill is just as vital, if not more so if you want to leave your organization than if you want to stay. The only way that you will discover organizations where you can successfully practise your change skills is by talking to people, reading books and articles and attending conferences. Networking will also give you the opportunity to display your new found skills. Once you have pinpointed the organizations that meet your requirements then you need to take the initiative to obtain a job with them. Again these are the skills of a change winner and we have covered them for you in chapter 7.

Uncomfortable with the type of change on-going in your organization?

This lack of comfort could fall into two categories. Either you do not like the change process itself or you are not happy with the planned outcomes. Is change in your organization being driven top-down by senior managers with little or no opportunity for you to take part? Conversely, the change process could involve the total empowerment of staff and restructuring into self-managed teams. Yet you are uncomfortable with the role of facilitator and coach. You may be happier with a lower degree of involvement such as suggestion or job involvement as described in chapter 6.

199

In some circumstances, you may not be sure whether you are comfortable with either the process or the outcome but you can test what it feels like before making your decision whether to abandon ship or not. However, in other circumstances the risks associated with the outcome could be so great that you have no option but to leave. For example if there were 50 middle managers at the same level as you but in the new downsized structure there are only going to be five. Unless somebody has given some pretty concrete assurances that one of those jobs is yours, then you should be reaching for the life jacket. Change winners can turn even this gloomy scenario into an opportunity by planning a great new career plus collecting their redundancy check.

To find your ideal conditions you will need to follow the process outlined above although the outcome you will be seeking is different.

Change lover seeking exciting possibilities

Some people discover that they can really thrive on change. They see the attributes of a change winner and they realize that they are almost as natural to them as breathing. Either because they have developed these skills through past experience or because many of them were natural strengths that they have honed and developed. Change winners did not realize they could be winners in previous, stable environments where command, control and position based power ruled the day. They were often considered somewhat counter-cultural with their participative management style and their emphasis on development and calculated risk taking. In the new world of change, change and more change, those skills once considered rather suspect are greatly in demand.

So what do you do if you love change? You could either pour all your energies into bringing about change either as an internal or external management consultant or you could combine elements of change management with other aspects of your previous jobs that you enjoyed by developing a portfolio career.

Change losers

We are sure that none of you personally fall into this category but you will know many colleagues and a few friends who do. What can you advise them? Many of them have been or even still are extremely successful at command and control and do not want to or find it difficult to give up. The different types can be found in the organizational safari park. There are the lumbering dinosaurs who still feel they rule the planet and do not realize that extinction awaits them. Then there are the fearsome tigers. They understand that their number is diminishing but they will survive because they are the best of their breed. The ostriches have their heads firmly buried in the sand. They have seen change initiatives come and fail in the past, why should now be any different? If change is perceived as being inescapable they just dig their heads even deeper.

Some final thoughts

Now hopefully you are a change winner and want to share your success with those facing change in the future. A way to do that is to ensure that this book remains a live document and is updated not only by our experience through the often stormy passages of change but also yours. We would welcome input from you covering not only the pinnacle of your success but also the darkest depths of your failures. This way we can ensure that our profile of a change winner remains valid and can continue to act as a beacon for those chartering the seas of change. We have illustrated this book with case studies from our own experience and those researched from the literature but in future updates it would be valuable to use examples of efforts of previous readers. This will certainly help future readers along the path to success.

However, if you are not quite a change winner yet and find yourself in danger of sinking and cannot find the lifejacket readily available in the book, then also contact us because we need to extend our toolkit of ideas and hints for future editions and perhaps we can give you a helping hand. We can be contacted at:

Quadra Consulting
Mary Sheridan House
St. Thomas' Street
London
SE1 9RS

Telephone: 0171 955 8851/2
Fax: 0171 955 4856

Index

■ ■ ■